RICHARD ATTENBOROUGH'S CHORUS LINE

⋆ *Richard Attenborough's* ⋆
CHORUS LINE

Compiled by Diana Carter
Photographs by Josh Weiner and Alan Pappé

ACADEMIC PRESS CANADA
in association with
THE BODLEY HEAD

British Library Cataloguing
in Publication Data
Attenborough, Richard
and Carter, Diana
I. Title
782.81 PN1997.C46

ISBN 0 7747 0138 2
Printed in Great Britain for
The Bodley Head Ltd
30 Bedford Square, London WC1B 3RP
by W.S. Cowell, Ipswich
Set in Rotation by Text Filmsetters Ltd
First published 1985

Filming 'A Chorus Line'

by Richard Attenborough

It was Marti Baum's idea ...
I am not sure there are many people who would have thought it a good one, but Marti, who is my agent in Los Angeles, was convinced he had two good reasons why I should accept the offer to direct *A Chorus Line*. Firstly, that I had an eye and an ear for a musical. This he'd believed since he saw the first film I directed, *Oh! What a Lovely War*. His second reason was more pragmatic. He believed that, in career planning, I should take on a subject which unlike my previous film, *Gandhi*, did not have the major social connotations with which I had come to be associated.

I have to admit to thinking he was somewhat dotty. I had already decided that my next film would be set in South Africa, attempting to examine life in that country under the obscenity of apartheid.

There were a number of other possibilities also being mooted in the summer of '83. One concerned a major historical British romantic figure and another was a fascinating project involving Diana Ross, for whom I have always had an enormous admiration.

But Marti was persistent. 'Well, at least why don't you come over to see the show? It must be four or five years since the London run. You probably don't remember it all that well.'

He was right. I had seen a production at the Theatre Royal Drury Lane in the late Seventies and although I had enjoyed it tremendously had certainly never envisaged the possibility of it being made into a movie.

I talked it over with my wife, Sheila, and she agreed that it would be a good idea to avoid being considered as a director of only one particular *genre* of film. And, since both of us have unqualified faith in Marti's judgement, it was arranged that I'd go to New York to meet the producers, Cy Feuer and Ernie Martin.

Cy and Ernie came to see me at the Regency Hotel on the morning after my arrival and we bought tickets to see the show together that night.

I remember going to the theater with this intense feeling of anticipation. I was certain that it was going to be massively entertaining, but what I did not realise was the extent to which I would be bowled over by the show, by its wonderful theatricality, the originality of its

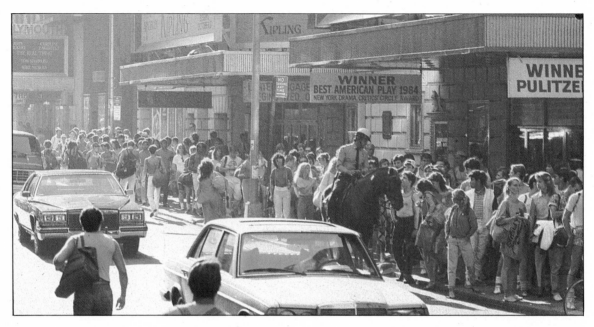

Dancers line up to attend a 'cattle call' on Broadway

concept and, perhaps most impressive of all, by the discipline and commitment displayed by the entire company.

A Chorus Line is about casting a forthcoming Broadway musical. Zach, the director/choreographer, is seeking eight dancers, four boys and four girls, to make up the chorus. He will choose them from literally hundreds of 'gypsies', as they call themselves, attending an open audition known, aptly but cruelly, as the 'cattle call'. Hundreds of young people, all desperately seeking work, are taught a 'combination' of dance steps and given a few seconds to display their talent before being summarily rejected or chosen to remain for further eliminations. Finally, just sixteen are left and, before selecting the final eight, Zach requires them all to reveal their personalities in order to judge who may also be capable of playing some small parts. The tension is aggravated by the arrival of Cassie, the dancer who loved – and left – Zach some time ago. She, too, wants to join 'the line' and audition for the show.

The music is outstanding and several of the numbers – 'What I Did for Love', 'At the Ballet' and 'One' – have become classics in their own right. The score, of course, is by Marvin Hamlisch and the lyrics by Ed Kleban. After a number of discussions with Cy and Ernie, it was agreed that they would write two new numbers for the movie, 'Surprise, Surprise' and 'Let Me Dance for You'. It seems to me that both are destined to be enormous hits.

That first evening on Broadway I was immensely moved by several moments in the show. I remember particularly that when Maggie, one of the dancers, recalling her childhood, said, 'Daddy, I would love to dance,' tears rolled down my face in complete abandonment to sheer theatrical magic.

The audience was totally captivated. You could have heard a pin drop during the dramatic scenes and their enjoyment of the music and humor was manifest.

The production was wonderful and I did feel that it could be transferred to the screen. What worried me was that Michael Bennett's brilliant conception, of setting the action in the theater and not departing from it at all, appeared intrinsic to its very success. What should the cinematic form be? Would a story set on a bare stage and in an empty auditorium satisfy a movie audience? Perhaps one ought to examine very carefully the possibility of moving away from the theater and using the kids' revelations as narration for a series of illustrative flashbacks. Certainly, the Zach/Cassie relationship could be re-examined. But might not tampering with that also risk destroying the original dynamic?

I had read Arnold Schulman's initial screenplay, and he had decided with some minimal exceptions to remain in the theater. I thought some of his dialog adhered too strictly to the play and, in addition, was concerned that a certain number of what I'll call flashbacks might place the Bennett concept in jeopardy. Arnold is a very flexible writer and we set about examining the various problems in detail once I had conveyed my reservations to Cy and Ernie.

Feuer and Martin are part of the very fabric of Broadway. Their list of credits, in terms of American musical shows, makes up theater history even if one only mentions, among many others, *How to Succeed in Business Without Really Trying* and *Guys and Dolls*. Their principal venture into movies with *Cabaret* (again involving Marti Baum, then in charge of A.B.C. Films) was a phenomenal success.

Cy and Ernie are a classic duo in every sense. Ernie must be six feet tall and wears glasses. He's quite thin and he seems to insinuate his way around a room, behind a desk, into a car. Cy can't be much more than five foot six and moves with a pugnacious determination. Whereas Ernie is absolutely upright, Cy lists forward at forty-five degrees, permanently about to pounce. Whether every great creative team is made up of one long and one short, I don't know, but certainly every comedic couple of any quality benefits from such physical disparity, and Cy and Ernie, in providing constant amusement, proved no exception.

Arnold Schulman

The question of relationships, of characterisation, of dynamic, of narrative line, is always an element which occupies a great deal of the writer's and the director's attention, and in this particular instance, of course, the producers' as well. The four of us had innumerable script conferences. They ranged over a vast number of topics, from the detail of a particular line of dialog to major considerations of structure. We concluded, for instance, that our flashbacks, no matter what their subject matter, should also carry the sound of what is happening in the theater. In this way, although they take longer for us to display than a mere flash in the character's recall, we always retain the atmosphere and tension of the actual audition.

Selecting the technicians who will work on the film during production, plus those involved in the editing department during post-production, is a primary task of any producer/director team. Fortunately, Cy and Ernie were content that I should have the final say in their assembly.

However, there was one particular function, absolutely crucial to the making of *A Chorus Line* and which would largely determine its style, of which I had no experience whatsoever and on which I had to be guided by Cy. That was the position of choreographer.

We had agreed, with Ernie, that if the movie was to have any chance at all, it simply had to have a contemporary image. And that not only meant casting people who were in their teens and early twenties, but also displaying choreography essentially of today.

Cy had in mind someone with whom he'd worked on a number of occasions over the years and spoke of him in the most glowing terms. However, out of the blue, he saw a film called *Flashdance* and, bearing in mind our discussions, began to revise his opinion. I went with him to a matinée showing and, from the moment it started, found myself in complete agreement with Cy's change of heart. The manner, form, style of dance were extraordinary. Even with my lack of previous experience, I felt sure we had found the perfect choreographer.

His name was Jeffrey Hornaday and I was to discover that he was still only twenty-seven years old, the same age as my youngest child, Charlotte.

Our first meeting was over lunch at Sardi's. Jeffrey proved to be slightly willowy in one sense and yet evidently possessed of enormous physical strength and agility. He has a curtain of almost white-blond hair which requires his constant attention. His dress is a wonderment. Studied carelessness, one of Noël Coward's favorite descriptions, is, when applied to Jeffrey, an understatement of monumental proportions. His clothes look as if he's slept in them for a week and any suggestion that they might fit in any direction would be a total denial of their very style.

The fact that he's still so young and utterly brilliant is enough to drive anyone nuts! I don't think I've encountered a potentially greater talent in the forty years I've been in the business. His feeling for style and tempo, his understanding of film, his musical know-

Jeffrey Hornaday

ledge, his invention and vision are quite remarkable. The empathy between us was immediate. Our taste seemed to coincide almost intuitively.

Together with Cy and Ernie, Jeffrey and I agreed that the prime qualification for casting should be dance. Because so much of the dancing involves the whole line, there was no chance of making a satisfactory film unless they were all capable of the very highest standards. And so, echoing *A Chorus Line* itself, we held open auditions as well as Screen Actors' Guild calls.

The sight outside the Royale Theater in New York at nine o'clock on the first morning was amazing. Boys and girls had been waiting since the early hours and the line, four and five abreast, must have been seventy or eighty yards long.

Many, in this open call, were highly professional people. But there were also, inevitably, the characters, the kooks. One particular person, I remember, came dressed in a brown bearskin, including the head, and absolutely refused to remove it. He or she, needless to say, was not called back. But many were.

Even to an untrained eye like mine, it was very quickly evident who was competent and who was not. Every now and again, somebody just leapt out from all the others and was immediately, therefore, not only called back but placed on a list to be considered for a particular part.

This went on for several days. We then repeated the same process, the same fining down, in Los Angeles. I found it an exhilarating experience but also a very

Underneath the camera crane on a New York street

Cy Feuer and Ernest Martin

distressing one. Being an actor, one is conscious of just what auditions, in any form, mean to the person concerned. If you are offering your painting or your book or your piece of typing, that is an article which is either accepted or rejected. If you are auditioning as a performer, you undergo personal acceptance or rejection.

I remember in Los Angeles there was a child, a girl, who, having been 'cut' – told she was no longer required – came rushing over to ask why. Jeffrey, wanting to be kind, suggested that perhaps she was a little too young. 'But I can look much older,' she said and ran to produce some photographs which certainly did add a few years. So we asked her to come back, both knowing that it wasn't her age but her dancing that was lacking.

By then we were auditioning people in groups of six or eight, and of course she had to be cut again. Everyone left the centre of the studio except this child who stood there, alone and absolutely still. Suddenly tears coursed down her cheeks and, grabbing her dance bag from a chair, she careered out of the studio door. I followed her, terrified she'd run under a car.

With some of the crew (left to right): B.J. Bjorkman, Jeffrey Hornaday, Bob Girolami, Eddie Quinn, Ronnie Taylor, Tom Priestley, Cy Feuer, Michael White and Michael Tronick

She was all right. But that was just one example of the emotional strain and despair that can totally enshroud a young person, particularly one without much experience, during an audition. I couldn't forget this particular girl and asked Arnold Schulman if he'd put something similar in the script, and she became 'the girl in yellow trunks', for all to see. The quality of any film emanates unquestionably from the screenplay. *A Chorus Line* is no exception and whatever success it achieves is, in no small measure, due to Arnold's undoubted skill.

Finally, after seeing over three thousand dancers, we got down to about four hundred from whom we would select the hundred and twenty for the big opening sequence and some of the seventeen who would make up 'the line'.

Slowly we refined these into a smaller group, gave them scenes to learn and re-auditioned them as actors and actresses. We then decided that approximately sixty justified a screen test. I was very anxious that this should be a fully fledged operation, believing it was impossible to make a proper judgement on video. I felt we should have a first-rate cameraman and crew shooting on 35mm Panavision in a desire to give the kids – the vast majority of whom had never worked in film before – every possible opportunity of displaying their talents to the full.

A Chorus Line is, of course, an American subject. It is also an American film. And consequently one assumed that the crew, as well as the cast, would be indigenous.

I had always envisaged having an American director of photography but, for various reasons, the studio was unable to make a firm commitment early enough to secure the person I had in mind. By then, other American lighting cameramen who might have been appropriate for this particular project were also committed. So my thoughts went to the possibility of a British director of photography and back to *Gandhi*.

Ronnie Taylor and I understand each other. We have a similar point of view and no one is more creative or devoted to the job in hand than he. I put forward his name to Cy, Ernie and the studio and, in the knowledge

Trying to emulate the dancers with, behind, 'the girl in yellow trunks'

Ronnie Taylor

that Ronnie had won the Oscar jointly with Billy Williams in 1983, there really was next to no discussion.

The other Oscar winner who I very much wanted to be part of the team was the editor of *Gandhi*, John Bloom. He was free to accept the assignment and, since it was always my intention to cut the film in England, it made absolute sense to have a British editor. John also happens to be brilliant at his job.

The camera operator is a vital figure in any director's life. Minute by minute, hour by hour, day by day, one probably works even more closely with him than with the lighting cameraman. Everyone I knew with experience of working in New York begged me to try to secure the services of Tom Priestley. Thank God, I was fortunate enough to do so, for he is superb. Tom is taciturn, absolutely mesmerised by the particular shot he is helping to create and, if given to an irascible moment here and there, follows it, almost immediately, by demonstrating a most engaging, sly sense of humor.

Our splendid associate producer, Joe Caracciolo, had worked with production designer Patrizia von Brandenstein on a number of movies and recommended her highly. There is no denying it, she is a galleon. Nearly six feet tall, she sails into a room, carrying herself like an empress. She also has a marvelous sense of humor which, most of the time, she tries to disguise in an attempt to convince you she's a highly serious, committed, creative member of the team which, undoubtedly, she is. We were all thrilled when she won her Oscar for *Amadeus*.

Setting up for the big opening number

Jeffrey rehearsing with Alyson Reed who plays Cassie

As with Tom Priestley, our sound recordist was someone much praised by everyone who'd previously worked in New York. His name is Chris Newman and he, too, is of the very highest caliber. His virtually unique adaptability and ingenuity while we were shooting were hugely beneficial to the finished picture.

New York gypsies have a very special style about them and, bearing in mind the youthful appeal of the film, costume was one of the elements through which this image could be projected. Ernie suggested Faye Poliakin as a costume designer, who had primarily been involved until then with MTV as against cinema – but her eye was terrific and her contribution very considerable.

For the director, another of the key people on the floor is the script supervisor, who keeps a continuity record of just about everything to do with the actual shooting. 'B.J.' Bjorkman came to the production with a stunning reputation. She is a tall, witty, very good-looking woman who helped to establish and maintain an atmosphere of excitement, wonderment and joy in the creation of a motion picture. Everyone, cast and crew alike, adored her.

Rehearsals were terrific, one of the most enjoyable experiences I've had in my life. Organised by the warm-hearted Phil Friedman, they lasted eight weeks and were primarily intended for the creation of choreography. It was marvelous to be a part of that process and, as I had anticipated, Jeffrey and I got on like a house on fire. We were tremendously fortunate in having Brad Jeffreys as assistant choreographer, Bob Wooten as drummer and Joseph Joubert, a pianist/composer of such talent that the newly devised dance sections could be rehearsed and filmed against music which echoed the mood and style of Jeffrey's work.

I was massively impressed by the kids' dedication. They are a unique breed, these dancers/singers/actors/actresses. Indigenous to the United States, they require themselves to have a compilation of all three disciplines. Inevitably, they may shine more in one than the others, but nevertheless the triumvirate of talent is assumed. They work phenomenally hard. Their preparation – dance classes, gymnasium work, voice training, and so on – is continually maintained within the constraints of working at their profession and they have an unqualified commitment to the job in hand.

By the time we were ready to leave the Minskoff Rehearsal Rooms for the ambience of the Mark Hellinger Theater, the move itself released a massive charge of adrenalin and we started shooting on 1 October, 1984 with the whole cast almost incapable of containing their excitement.

Principal photography began with the big opening audition number which occurs a few minutes into the film and with what came to be known as 'the pigeon shot'. I wanted very much to start on a close-up, actually his first, of Zach and then pull the camera back at enormous speed over the heads of all the dancers cramming the stage. During early discussions, one of the crew was heard to mutter darkly that the only way it

Alyson with our gaffer, Dick Quinlan, and, holding the light meter, Ronnie Taylor

could be done was to attach the camera to a pigeon's backside and have it fly across the theater. Eventually we managed – without the pigeon – by using a zoom lens and, with the crew, stripped almost down to their underwear, pushing the camera on its dolly faster than I ever believed possible. But the shot works and it was well worth the effort.

It is customary in musicals to pre-record the final vocal track of any number and a scratch or temporary instrumental track – the two being separate – before you begin shooting. When you actually come to film,

the artist synchronises his or her lip movements to the existing song for every camera set-up. It seemed to me, however, that for certain numbers we should dispense with this supposedly essential mode of operation. Being to an extent the amateur, I suppose it was somewhat cocky of me to insist. But I can honestly say that the final result was eminently worthwhile. The fact that two of the principal songs were recorded for the first time while we were actually shooting and then used immediately as the guide track, has resulted, I believe, in a spontaneity of performance and a degree of passion created in

Watching the instant replay of a dance sequence on video (left to right): Audrey Landers, Gregg Burge, Jan Gan Boyd, Tony Fields, Pam Klinger, Jeffrey Hornaday, Justin Ross, Michael Blevins, Michelle Johnston, Michael White and Ronnie Taylor

Informality could be translated into concentration

front of the camera which would have been impossible in the clinical atmosphere of the recording booth.

Shooting lasted some sixteen weeks and progressed similarly, I think, to any movie except for difficulties peculiar to this production. If you are working in virtually the same setting, day after day, week after week, it can, to say the least, become somewhat monotonous. In addition, to facilitate the sound department, the theater had been sealed off from the outside to prevent extraneous noise, and this, with only a rather questionable ventilation system in operation, was undoubtedly debilitating. If you add that the same seven-

teen people lined up in the same clothes in exactly the same order facing the camera for several months on end, you can imagine the whole atmosphere could become pretty oppressive. However, by a mixture of tomfoolery and informality, capable, when necessary, of being translated into absolute concentration, I believe we avoided that pitfall.

Certainly the kids were tired, really tired, by the end of the schedule. Certainly there were little moments of irritation that crept in as a result. But, in the main, the atmosphere on the floor was terrific. This was created and maintained, in no small measure, by the

With editor John Bloom and, in the background, Michael Blevins

assistant directors. The first assistant, Bob Girolami, is superb at his job and had been highly recommended at the outset. Both I and the production owe him a considerable debt for the perception with which he anticipated the capability of the unit and therefore our ability to adhere to the schedule. His assistant, Louis Esposito, and the various other ADs, trainees and production assistants were also immensely supportive and they were greatly aided by stalwart New York technicians such as Dick Quinlan, the gaffer, Eddie Quinn, the key grip, Jack Volpe, the dolly grip, and Joe Caracciolo Jr., the master propman.

Art directors, sketch artists, scenic artists, stills cameramen, hairdressers, make-up artists, wardrobe masters and mistresses, electricians, carpenters, painters, set-dressers, construction grips, security men...all contribute to the making of a movie. As indeed do the backroom people: the production office, the accounts department, the publicity department, the personal assistants and the drivers.

No one person makes a film. There are *auteur* directors who dominate a production without paying much heed to anybody else's opinion. That is not my way. I enjoy, as it were, being the conductor of an

With Jeffrey and some of the dancers who filled the stage for the finale

orchestra; but one which has its various leaders in each section. All make their separate and valuable contribution to the final result. To work with our New York crew was both a pleasure and a privilege.

There was, at the outset, a lack of unanimity regarding the film's finale. I felt very strongly that, if the story had achieved its intended climax emotionally, to follow that moment by merely re-introducing the same cast who had been on the screen for two hours would inevitably result in anti-climax.

What I had in mind was a fairly expensive operation. The whole finale had to be staged in a moment of abstract sleight of hand. The set had to change, yet remain the same. The kids had to change, yet remain the same. And the costumes had to have all the glitz and glamor of a Broadway spectacular. Ultimately, I was able to persuade not only Cy and Ernie but also the owners of Embassy Pictures, Gerry Perenchio, Norman Lear and Alan Horn, that the additional expenditure was justified.

So the movie ends in a blaze of gold satin and glittering sequins with more and more chorus appearing on the stage and adding their voices, as if by magic, to the words of 'One' in our heartfelt tribute to every gypsy who ever danced on Broadway.

In this souvenir book, which echoes the format of *A Chorus Line* itself, each of the film's twenty featured players talks about their own lives and the parts they play in the movie. I have added my own comments.

Michael Blevins

MARK

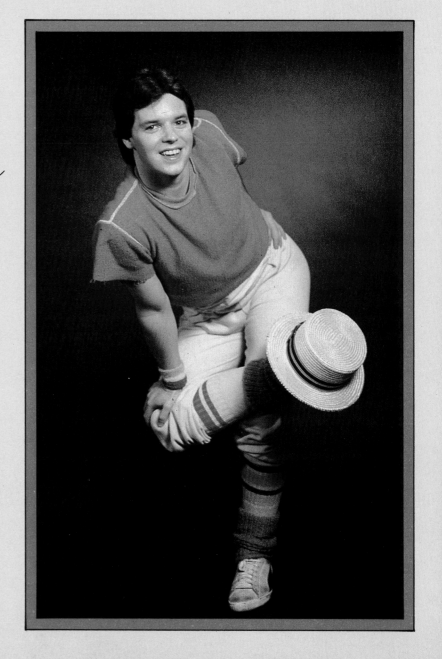

Broadway
Bring Back Birdie (Mike)
Little Me (Arthur)
The Tap Dance Kid (Winslow Alexander)

Off-Off-Broadway
Bags (Dealer)
Time Pieces
FIT Industrial

Television
The Nashville Palace (featured performer), ABC TV

Stock
Cabaret (Emcee)
Fiddler on the Roof
Godspell (Jesus)
Opryland USA

Special Skills
Juggling, choreography, gymnastics, piano, guitar

When I left, I was in a strange state of mind. I was walking in the street and I thought, 'You'd better pay attention or you're going to get hit by a car.' I had just done my screen test for *A Chorus Line* with Richard. Beforehand, we just talked and then ran the scene a little between us. He read Zach's lines and I did mine. Then he said, 'That was good. Would you like to do it now? Or do you want another rehearsal?'

I was like, 'What do you mean? You're the director. Don't ask me.' So I said, 'Let's just do it,' and he said, 'Fine.'

They only made me do it once and Richard said it was perfect and just what he wanted and they're all shaking my hand. So I guessed that was a good sign. I still didn't know. They wouldn't tell me. But it felt kind of good and, like I said, I walked out of there in this strange state of mind.

I like living in New York a whole lot, but sometimes I get really depressed because of all the violence and crime.

While we were filming the movie, I got mugged on a Saturday night. They didn't get much – only about ten dollars – but it was scary. I'd gone to get a pack of cigarettes and it was very late. Maybe two-thirty or three in the morning. I turned a corner and there was this bunch of five guys. I didn't feel nervous or anything and just kept walking through the group. One of them bumped into me, put his arm round my throat and cut off my circulation. The others started rummaging through my pockets until finally I passed out. That was probably lucky because they thought they'd killed me. So they got scared and ran off.

I guess you could say I used to be pretty naïve. When I came to New York I thought that Broadway was the name of just one theater. And Radio City ... I'd never heard it called the Music Hall so I decided it would be kind of neat to live there and asked if there were any apartments to rent.

Mark, the character I play in the movie, is young, eager and kind of naïve, too. He's probably attending his very first audition. I don't think he cares how long it goes on or even if he'll get paid for the job. He just wants to be given the opportunity to dance in the chorus.

I began taking dance lessons when I was five – the only boy in the whole school. For the first couple of years I took all the classes. Then I refused to take ballet and jazz because I thought they were 'sissy'. But tap and gymnastics, they seemed kind of okay and cool.

What I really wanted was to be an actor. I didn't realise for a very long time that people were actually paid for performing. Then one day my mother said something about how much you could earn from TV commercials. And I was amazed. I really and truly believed that they did it for fun. That was why I did it.

The first professional job I ever had was at a dinner theater, where people eat and watch a show at the same time, in Johnson City, Tennessee. They needed chorus people, dancers, for a production of *Fiddler on the Roof*. I was sixteen years old and had just got my driver's license which was really handy because

the place was about fifteen miles from our home.

This proved to be a really hard time because I was going to school in the day, then directing some young kids in a play and right after that had just forty-five minutes to drive to the dinner theater. I'd be home around midnight. Then I did my homework, which took another two or three hours. I started getting all these headaches, really bad migraines. I just wasn't getting enough sleep. But I still loved it and couldn't believe they were actually paying me thirty-five dollars a week.

I certainly wouldn't live in New York now if my business didn't call for it. But with this movie and the job I had before in the Broadway show, *The Tap Dance Kid*, I've earned enough money to fix up my apartment the way I want with dance mirrors.

I once had about nine months between shows and financially things got a little bit hairy. I know my parents would never let me starve. If it came down to that I could call and say, 'Mom, I need my rent.'

But I've never had to ask them for money since I moved out at sixteen and never really suffered. I've been on unemployment which, at first, I didn't want to accept. I thought I didn't deserve it. A bright, intelligent person shouldn't need cash that's meant for really poor people. Then I thought some more and realised that I'd paid my dues when I was working and I should take it.

That's what I'll do between *A Chorus Line* and my next job. I'll go down and collect unemployment.

*M*ark was one of the more difficult parts to cast. First of all, at seventeen, he's the youngest member of the cast and needs to be very ingenuous in a way which is acceptable in the mid-Eighties which is, inevitably, different from what was acceptable when the show opened a decade earlier. This ingenuousness has to be real. If it isn't, then his reactions to Zach's questioning and his blatant anxiety to be chosen become somewhat nauseating, not only to the rest of 'the line', which is correct, but to us in the audience, which is wrong.

Secondly, Mark has to lead off the sequence 'Hello Twelve' which recalls the first sexual awakening and awareness in a teenage boy or girl. This has to be achieved with frankness and simplicity which avoid it becoming merely smutty.

All those things Michael, or Blevins, as I call him, manages. I would think he has a real career ahead of him. He wants to know everything that's going on and loves the other side of the camera. He is also a very good actor and I understand from Jeffrey that he's also an excellent dancer. His acting is intuitive. He works very hard and was totally prepared both for his audition and, much more importantly, for when he was playing. He was absolutely at concert pitch and the only problem throughout the movie was, in fact, to hold him down, to persuade him that he didn't have to do a tap dance or wave his arms around to gain attention and register his character. He couldn't quite believe he could just *be*.

Yamil Borges

MORALES

Broadway
West Side Story (Rosalia)

Off-Broadway
El Bravo (Mariana) *Transposed Heads* (Sita)

Television
Fame (Dancer), TV Pilot ABC
Tony Awards (singer/dancer)
NYU Film, Monedas (principal)
Industrial Study, Xerox (principal)
Extra Work: *Guiding Light*, *One Life to Live*, *Ryan's Hope*

Regional Theater
Kismet (Princess of Ababu)
Sound of Music (singer/dancer)
West Side Story (singer/dancer)

Revues
Bally's Park Place, Atlantic City, NJ
Royal York Hotel, Toronto, Ontario
Club Ibis, New York, NY
Ted Hook's On Stage, New York, NY

*T*he first time Sir Richard saw me I was walking on crutches.

Three days before my dance audition and first reading for him, I was rehearsing a play and really immersed in this improvisation. I remember feeling so glad I was an actress and could let out all my emotions. I was oblivious to what I was doing and stamped my foot on a radiator pipe that was sticking out of the floor. They rushed me to the hospital and, in the emergency room, I'm screaming, 'I have an audition for the movie *A Chorus Line*. I can't have my foot all stitched up like this. Please, someone help me!'

Mind you, I think I was still able to look sexy when I met him. I put on my tights and my little grey suede boots with the little spiky heels and I walked through the city on crutches. Luckily enough, they didn't call on me to dance until a month later and my foot was better.

I love Sir Richard. It seems as though I have loved him forever and known him forever. Maybe people will think it's funny, but I look at him and I think my roots, wherever they may be, must be entwined with his somewhere. I look at him and I know; maybe in another place, another time ... I just feel so much a part of him.

I was born in San Lorenzo, Puerto Rico, near the rain forests, and came to New York when I was very young where I was raised in the Bronx. I only met my real father twice so, if and when I have lots of money, I'm going to have someone dig up my roots. I have had two stepfathers who were brothers. My mother had a set of twins by each of them, one set of boys and one of girls. They're fraternal, not identical.

I'm a Gemini – the sign of the twins – which is really ironic. I told my mother, 'Well, you really had three sets of twins because I'm like two people all rolled into one.'

It's not like I ever decided to be an actress. It's my existence. It's the essence of me to perform.

When I was in junior high school, the guidance counsellor called me down one day and said that we had to sign papers to say which high school I wanted to attend. I don't know how, but somewhere in the back of my mind was the High School of Performing Arts.

So I tried out as an actress and as a dancer. I had no idea of what an audition was. I was turned down for drama but, thank God, I also auditioned for the dance department and was accepted.

I grew up where there were black Latin people. It was a ghetto. Not a ghetto in the sense of a slum, dirty, filthy, deteriorating. It could be that. The South Bronx was known for that. But where I lived was a ghetto in the sense that it was home to a certain type of culture and nationality.

Then I went to Performing Arts on 46th Street with girls who were German, girls who were Irish, Italian, and girls who'd arrive in the morning wearing fur coats. There were people who were dropped at school in limousines.

Fame was about Performing Arts and, let me tell

you, Performing Arts could very well be that crazy. We lived in a world of our own. I mean we're talking about six inches of snow and you'd see little ballerinas in their satin slippers crossing the street to get a hero sandwich from the deli on the corner and New Yorkers looking at us as if we were nuts.

Afterwards my stepfather was determined to send me to Community College but I didn't want to go, so I ran away from home. For two years I worked selling men's clothing on the lower East Side of Manhattan. Sometimes I'd do pirouettes in the middle of the floor and the manager would have a fit. I was just so miserable, it came out of my pores. I looked ugly, my complexion was bad, my eyes had no light, no shine and I was very young and exploited in a way I don't even want to talk about.

One day I said to myself, I don't care if I starve, I'm going to quit this store and selling clothing to these people and I'm going back into show business.

And I did. I went hungry for a while but then I auditioned for Club Ibis. I started out in the chorus and left as the lead and went straight into my first Broadway show.

My mother and stepfather were very hurt when I ran away but I'll never forget my opening night on Broadway when I took my family to Sardi's. I'd saved money and bought my mother the prettiest clothes. I said, 'Daddy, you order whatever you want.' My stepfather was looking at the menu prices and asking, 'Are you sure?'

I said, 'Daddy, I ordered the best champagne...' He had *filet mignon*. He was beaming with joy.

And I told him, 'You see, Daddy, you see ... I knew what I wanted. You just had to give me a chance. I'm a bird. I just need to fly.'

By the time I'm, say, forty I want to be in a situation where my family has everything they need. So that my mother will see the good things in life and not lie awake at night and wonder whether the Welfare is going to take her money away. To me, my mother is a queen. I want to be able to offer my brothers and sisters an opportunity to see the world and, above all, I want to portray Latin people very positively, with a lot of dignity and grace.

I would like to have a husband some day. I really and truly would like to be married. But I'm so critical, and I'm so fickle, too. I wonder if I'm ever going to be able to live with anyone else. I've lived with a guy, but I need an environment that is very peaceful and serene because I'm totally the opposite. I do get very lonely, but the important things in life are good friends, family you can depend on and faith. I believe in God, so I'm never really alone.

Paris was very lonely for me. I went there with *West Side Story*, playing Rosalia which was a chorus contract, but I understudied Anita and got to play her twice while the company was in France.

On Christmas Eve I called America to wish my stepfather Merry Christmas. He had been dead a month and I didn't know... My first stepfather was murdered

on 24 December when I was seven.

And then during *A Chorus Line* my number, where I sing 'Nothing', was due to be filmed on Christmas Eve.

I told Sir Richard, 'Three years ago, when I heard my second stepfather had died, I would never have dreamed that this could happen, that my life could change so much and I would do something wonderful on this date.'

It turned out that we didn't film it until later. But I wouldn't have minded if it had been that day because I'd have been singing for my father and I'd have known he was listening to me.

Diana Morales, the part I play in the movie, is me ... or I am her. She wants what is rightfully hers. An opportunity to be whatever she wants to be and an opportunity to perform. She's tough and if she has to kick some ass, she'll kick some ass. But when she has to be sweet and loving and vulnerable she is that, too.

No matter how soon after dawn we arrived at the Mark Hellinger Theater, steeped in darkness before the full crew came in, up there on the stage in just a little pool of work light, would by Yaya. She had already done her dance class and was now lying on her back with exercise weights attached to her feet and in her hands, working to maintain her dance muscles at peak performance level.

She was the only person who did it and couldn't give a damn whether anyone else considered it eccentric or silly. You would think her professionalism and considerable experience, especially as a solo performer in night clubs, would, to a degree, have eradicated some of her nervousness. In fact, she was probably the most apprehensive member of the cast.

We planned a number of pre-recording dates for her big number, 'Nothing', but as each approached, she was demonstrably and unquestionably ill. Becoming convinced that this was psychosomatic, I eventually had to push her over the edge, to say we'd record it anyway and if it wasn't right we'd do it again.

Even in the recording booth, singing to the playback of her scratchtrack, she was shaking with nerves. But when she came to film the number, which could easily have been rather predictable, she translated those nerves into the most extraordinary emotional intensity. She got all the humor and the lightness and, by God, when she came to the end, the degree of feeling that she injected into the last chorus is nothing short of magnificent.

Because my own background was very secure, as was my relationship with my parents – the antithesis of what Yaya went through – I don't have those experiences and emotions to call upon as an actor.

The background which she has described makes her the most wonderful piece of casting for Morales. As with one or two others, I had to fight for Yaya. But it was certainly worth it. Her talent suffuses the screen.

Jan Gan Boyd

CONNIE

Film
Gimme an F (co-star), 20th-Century Fox

Regional Theater
The King and I (Little Eva), with Yul Brynner
Robin Hood (Lola — lead)
The Lone Ranger, (Sioux — lead)

Special Skills
Language (some Chinese), gymnastics, martial arts, Polynesian dance,
bellydance, mime, cheerleading, surf and ski, choreography,
drive a stick shift

When I was a little girl, children threw rocks at my brother because we spoke 'funny'. We'd just moved out of San Francisco to a suburb called Fremont, in a predominantly white neighborhood. Until then our parents had taught us to speak Cantonese at home. But after the kids threw the rocks at my brother they decided not to raise us like that and since then I haven't learned any Chinese. I can still understand a little, but I don't speak it fluently.

I was never really proud to be Chinese when I was younger, but since my father took me to the Cantonese village where he was born, when it was first possible in the late Seventies, I realised what a fantastic heritage I have and that China is an incredible country. It gave me a lot of pride in being Asian.

My father is a dentist and he wanted me, my brother and my two sisters to follow in his footsteps and have professions in the scientific world. So all four of us went to college. I wanted to be a therapist or some sort of psychologist. I got through four years and would have graduated in my fifth. Then I realised it wasn't what I really wanted to do. I decided it was either my happiness or what my father wanted me to be . . . I thought. But it worked out great because when I told my parents that I was going to be a dancer and that I'd gotten a job in *The King and I* with Yul Brynner they were really happy for me, and since I've been successful they've been very supportive.

Those four years of college helped me grow up, to get my head together, to discipline me, to help my concentration. I do like psychology a lot but I know now that dancing is my lifestyle and my work.

I started dancing when I was about five or six. My mother put me in ballet because I was such a clod. I'd fall over and hit my head all the time. So now I'm just a graceful clod.

I got married on 1st September 1984, while we were rehearsing for *A Chorus Line*. They let me go home during Labor Day weekend. I married John Boyd, a wonderful man who's studying to be a veterinarian at UC, Davis, which is where we met. We'd been dating for five years before we decided to get married. John is Caucasian with some American Indian in his family, way back. We're going to try and give our children a good sense of both heritages.

John came to New York with me for one week after we were married. Then he had to go back to school. It was difficult. I'd cry a lot and I'd get depressed because I was in a new city, and I didn't have my big, strong husband to take care of me and hold me at night.

I like to walk down the street and smile at people and you can't do that in New York. It's dangerous. I'm a very friendly and open person but I had to be very closed and reserved. I was in a hotel for two months and there were mice in my room which was horrendous. Then, one time, they locked me out. Another night Michelle Johnston and I were in the room and they checked in another set of people who used their key and just walked in on us. It was quite an eye-opener to move to New York and experience all that.

John knew that the movie was a high point in my career and his happiness when I got the part of Connie was mixed with anxiety and apprehension. He wouldn't have let me take the job if he thought it was going to hurt me, but he knew doing *A Chorus Line* would help me a lot. And we'd make money.

We are planning to start a family in a couple of years. When John graduates from Davis, we're thinking of living somewhere where he'd be happy, on the outskirts of Los Angeles, and I'd commute to work. When I get pregnant is when I go back to college to get my Master's degree in dance. Then, when I'm old and can't lift my legs any more, I would like to teach dance.

Connie Wong, the person I play in *A Chorus Line*, is very much like me, so it's easier to play it real. She's short and she's Asian and that makes her typecast. She's used to being turned down because she's too tiny or she's not white or she's not black. She tries hard but the only way she can get jobs and make people notice her is to try and play the part she thinks they want to see which is a cute little China doll.

When I'm under a lot of stress, when I feel very threatened and want to impress somebody, I turn into Connie Wong.

*J*ust before Jan left to get married, we had a collection amongst the cast and crew for a wedding present. We bought a pair of sapphire and diamond earrings and gave them to her with everyone gathered round for a send-off. When she opened the package and looked from the present to us, I knew I could get from Jan Gan Boyd what I wanted at the end of the movie.

She was absolutely bowled over. As Jan says herself, a lot of the time she plays Connie because that's how she copes professionally. But, as with all the characters, I wanted to delve deeper. I wanted to show what lies beneath the superficial performances that 'the line' put on for Zach's benefit in a way that is not possible in the stage play.

Connie reveals herself when she hears who has the job and who hasn't. We see how desperately it matters to her. And yet, earlier, when Zach asks what she's going to do when she can't dance any more, the answer is, 'Go off my diet and have babies.'

That is also very much Jan Gan Boyd, I think. She adores her chap, talks about him all the time and found the separation during shooting very hard. It is one of the problems that do beset young married couples in our business and it's very tough, even tougher if one person does something else.

To be a member of an ethnic minority is a strange feeling. It's very difficult for us to understand without going to Africa or Asia. I actually experienced it when I was making *The Sand Pebbles* in Taiwan. I remember being extremely self-conscious as one Caucasian amongst a sea of Chinese and comparatively, for the only time in my life, very tall.

Jan is small. I know how she feels.

Sharon Brown

KIM

Broadway
Joseph and the Amazing Technicolor Dreamcoat, (The Narrator - lead role)
Maggie Flynn (Violet Vandemere – principal child)

National Tour
Joseph and the Amazing Technicolor Dreamcoat, (The Narrator – lead role)
The Wiz (Dorothy – lead role)

Television
Love of Life (Daisy Allen – contract role)1½ yrs
Wish Upon a Star, Disney Cable Network
The Jeffersons (Louise Jefferson – age 15-18)
Good Times (Fun Girl – guest starring role)
Salt and Pepe (Nadeen – principal role), CBS Pilot

Variety TV
Merv Griffin Show, Johnny Carson Show
Midday with Bill Boggs, Toni Tennile Show
Sammy and Company, Macy's Thanksgiving Day Parade

Special Skills
Dialects: British, Southern, Heavy Brooklyn, Jewish, French
impersonations: Cher, Donna Summer, Dolly Parton,
Katherine Hepburn, Eva Gabor
horseback riding, skating (ice and roller), tennis,
swimming, writing and composing

Although this is my first movie, I've been working as a model, singer, writer, dancer and actress since I was a little girl. I started at three and a half, doing modelling and commercials. I made my Broadway debut at the age of five in *Maggie Flynn* with Shirley Jones and Jack Cassidy and I wasn't pushed into it.

My father is Johnny Brown from *Good Times* and *Laugh In* and nightclubs and commercials. My mother works in show business too although they didn't want it for me necessarily. But their friends used to say, 'Look, June, Johnny, you've got this kid here who wants to do what you're doing. Why don't you let her?'

And I kind of pulled them into it as if I was saying, 'Look at me, this is what I want to do, this is my business'.

I don't feel at all that I have lost any of my childhood. Think about children not in show business and having a so-called normal life who are being beaten and abused by their parents. I had a really normal childhood because my father and mother loved me to death and they love my brother to death. We're just a hugging family and we're a very close family. We're on the road a lot but we're always together. That's how I've been raised, along with very strong religious beliefs that have carried me through everything ... our business being so very shaky.

I was twenty-two when we made *A Chorus Line* and it seems to me that this society – and I don't know whether it's America or life in general – rushes you. Show business in particular pushes you to grow up quickly and do things early in life. I don't want to get married yet and I don't want to live with someone to get to know them. I've always wanted a husband and lots of children but I know I have to take my time. For a female especially there's a certain period in your life when you just can't do everything. You really have to pace yourself. That way, in the long run, I really believe you can do it all.

Show business is particularly difficult if you only have one talent. I'm very blessed because I have several. In *A Chorus Line* there are questions asked about what happens when you can't dance any more. Anyone in the world may have to face that. You can ask a doctor or a lawyer what happens to him or her when they can't practise. There is a threat in the film's story which is universal because it deals with dedication to a career, any career.

Gypsies are very special in the business because when you go to see a Broadway show and say, 'Wow! It's spectacular!' you're looking at the production numbers. It's the dancers who make those numbers exciting. Eight times out of ten the people who play the leads don't do much dancing. The gypsies always used to have the weakest union, the worst dressing-rooms and no one cared how they got on stage so long as they did get there. That's all changing now and I'm very glad. This is definitely the dancers' decade.

My part in *A Chorus Line*, compared to everyone else's, is relatively small. I've never seen the show. Playing Kim makes me feel very special because I'm not

stepping into a role that has been done on Broadway. She only exists in the film. Kim is Zach's secretary, his right arm, the one that sees all the tantrums and knows everything that's going on. I think Kim is a little snide at times because Zach will mess up or do something very silly and she'll just correct it without a blink. As if to say to this big guy, 'Look, this is really very simple.'

When I first auditioned, for some reason I didn't expect to see Sir Richard. When he came toward me I thought I wouldn't be able to walk. Usually, I don't get star-struck because I was raised around a lot of people who were famous. But when I saw him I went, 'Oh, my God,' and he must have seen that in my face because he took hold of my hand even though he was talking to another actor who was auditioning, and I stood there the entire time wondering how on earth was I going to get through this.

Finally he said, 'You're not nervous, are you?'

And I just told him. I felt the freedom to be honest and say, 'Look, I'm scared to death.'

One thing that stops my nerves is getting into a scene. The minute I turn into another character they vanish.

On the very first day I was shooting Sir Richard pulled me to one side and said, 'Let me tell you something, love, you didn't get the part because you're black or because you're attractive. It's because you're a damn good actress.'

And I said, 'Everybody should think that way. Black or white, if you can do the role you should get it.'

Casting sessions with Julie Hughes and Barry Moss are very rewarding. They are highly informed, immensely industrious and first-rate at their job. All our deliberations had an inherent variety of choice and none more so than when we came to cast Kim, created by Arnold Schulman for the movie. I felt that she should not be too much 'on the nail'. Julie and Barry asked if she could be black, Eurasian or Chinese. I had no preconceived ideas at all. I just wanted a girl who was attractive and efficient with a mind of her own rather than a conventionally brisk middle-aged woman or a dolly bird who was there merely because of good looks. Someone who could move between various areas of the theatre, as Arnold had envisaged certain scenes away from the stage itself, and someone who would also be a good foil for Zach.

I saw, I suppose, a dozen actresses. Finally I got down to two; one white and one black. But color had nothing to do with the final choice. It had to do with quality of personality because both girls were very, very good. I plumped for Sharon.

She is an excellent actress. She was apprehensive about making her first movie and playing a straight part. She's a marvelous singer and has made her name largely by virtue of that talent, but she brings everything I'd hoped to the part of Kim. She'll have problems, I think, in deciding which way her professional life is to go. But if she elects to put singing to one side and concentrate on acting, providing the parts are there, she'll have a very good career.

Gregg Burge

RICHIE

Film
The Cotton Club, Orion Pictures

Broadway
Sophisticated Ladies
The Wiz

Television
The Electric Company (series), PBS
Free To Be You and Me, ABC
Eubie Blake, a Century of Music, PBS
Young Artists at the White House, PBS
I Feel a Song Comin' On, PBS
Night of 100 Stars II, ABC

Off-Broadway
Bojangles
Evolution of the Blues

Choreography
One Mo' Time (off-Broadway), Asst. choreographer

Night Club
Les Mouches
Studio One/Backlit Theatre
Caesar's Palace, Atlantic City, NJ

Once I was awake the whole night. The movie was so important. So important to all of us. They had started to run behind schedule and I remember going through moments of fear that I wouldn't have enough time for my big number, 'Surprise', long enough to do it right.

Not being able to sleep at all was just terrible. That particular night I picked up the Bible and read the whole of *Psalms* and was still wide awake. There was a doctor who used to come by the theater and I asked him for a prescription. I didn't like asking for sleeping pills because I had always been against anything like that. I won't even take an aspirin. But I was beginning to feel so strange. I wanted sleep and peace of mind, to tune out everything and rest so that I could be in top form in the morning. Luckily in the end the problem resolved itself.

Richie, the part I play, is a young adult who exudes dance. His energy is so powerful that he cannot contain himself, literally cannot contain himself. Unless he tells somebody how much he loves to perform, then he's going to explode.

When we were shooting, I would get up at six which was pretty late, considering we had to be on stage by seven, seven thirty. It would take about an hour to wake up and take my shower. Then I'd go down to the theater, put my make-up on and warm up for another hour until they were ready for us. The hardest part is not to injure yourself when you dance for a shot and then stop. You have to be constantly warmed up. So instead of sitting down between shots, I'd continue to kick, stretch, split, whatever, knowing that, at any moment, they could call me back.

I had one dancing injury that seemed major at the time but it's fine now and doesn't hurt me at all. I was shooting the movie, *The Cotton Club*, only you won't see me in it because my part wound up on the editing room floor. I sprained my ankle on the last day. They told me I wouldn't dance for six weeks. And I was to open in Japan eight days later, playing the lead in the stage show of *Sophisticated Ladies*.

I just took it to the Lord Jesus and I said, 'Lord, you have to come through for me.'

So the next day I flew to Japan and they had doctors waiting for me at the airport. And they used acupuncture. On the opening night I danced with twelve fine needles like little coils in my ankle and continued to dance with them in for three more weeks. They killed the pain and took the swelling out.

I see myself as always dancing. Not always being able to do the steps that I can do now, but I don't think I'll ever get away from it and I wouldn't wish to. No other field in entertainment demands so much constant discipline, exercising every single day, starting with first position and then going to different levels which take you high and then off the ground. It's a feeling that you can't explain. To be able to control your legs and use them like ordinary people, everyone else, uses their arms. Without thinking about it.

I've know what I wanted to be since I was three. That was when I first saw Sammy Davis Jr. on TV.

I wanted to be the next Sammy Davis, to be in show business. A song and dance man. An actor. All of it. Seeing him was like a revelation. It really was. I knew that this was what I was going to do for the rest of my life. It was so clear to me. At three.

If my mother had been born a generation later, she would have been a concert pianist. But opportunities were not what they are today for black people. As a child in Alabama, she used to imagine herself playing the piano on a tin can because her parents couldn't even afford lessons. She got her piano as soon as we moved out to Long Island from Manhattan.

I remember it so clearly. At the time my father had a lot of bills and he asked if she could hold off. But as soon as we got the house, she bought it. My father came home and the piano was sitting there. I recall him being very annoyed and saying that they always did things together and that he'd asked her to wait and not buy it at this time because money was tight. And my mother said, 'You don't understand. This is something I just have to have.'

I understood. It was like the dance lessons I'd wanted when we couldn't afford them. She just couldn't wait any longer.

When I was ten I did my first commercial. It was for Mott's Clamato Juice: clams and tomato juice. After that I became a sort of king of commercials – we're going back fifteen years now to the time when they had to have one black in all of them. I was doing about thirty a year. A lot of my friends who worked as children have parents who went through all their money. It happens all the time. My parents saved two hundred thousand dollars for me and the funny thing was I didn't even know I was rich.

I remember one commercial experience in particular. The director said to the actress who was playing my mother, 'Could you read it a little more black, please?'

'I beg your pardon.'

'In the next take,' he said, 'could you do it a little more black?'

She told him, 'I am black. Now, if you want me to read it a little less articulated, then say so. But don't tell me to read more black.'

I've never forgotten that. So now when I'm up for a part I ask the casting people or the director about the character. I know he's black. But what else is he?

When they asked me to do a dance audition for *A Chorus Line* my pride was saying, 'Hey, wait a minute. You did your last Broadway show without auditioning.' And they told me, 'Well, Jeffrey Hornaday's from LA and he isn't up with the New York talent.'

And I thought, 'How dare they? I mean I'll sing and I'll act but I haven't had to do a dance audition for years.' But my agent said, 'You just go in and dance for him and shut up.'

So I did and it was the most fun audition I've ever taken. It was. I love Jeffrey's style. It works well on my body. Everyone else was tense and I was feeling so good. I remember Jeffrey's excitement when he was

watching me. I felt his vibrations coming at me. I knew he was on my side the moment I started dancing.

And then the third time, I knew that Richard was going to be there, watching us. I knew in my heart that the part was mine.

But there was competition, other people, and it depended on what type they were going for. I remem-ber when Richard walked into the room, the way he carried himself. And he smiled at me when I danced. He was just all teeth.

When I read Richie's first line, he laughed. Everyone laughed. He said, 'That's fun. Do it again.'

So I did it again and that's when I asked him, 'What is Richie's character like?'

And when he told me, I thought, 'Thank God. Here they're just going to let a person who is black be black and not have to play like society thinks he should.'

★ ★ ★

Gregg is a phenomenal dancer, without question the most remarkable dancer I've ever encountered directly in terms of work. I remember Jeffrey and I had no hesitation whatsoever in casting him as Richie as far as his dancing was concerned. We hadn't, at the time, heard the new number, 'Surprise', which Marvin Hamlisch and Ed Kleban were writing to replace 'Gimme the Ball' which Richie sings in the show.

It was changed, I think, for a couple of reasons. Ed, too, but Marvin particularly, felt that the original song, though good, wasn't a standout number. They also felt, I believe, as did everyone, that of all the songs in the show it was the most dated because it contained an element of tokenism. Ten or more years ago when 'Gimme the Ball' was written it made its own advance … limited though that was. Whereas now we needed something much more exciting and appropriate, much less 'Uncle Tom'. And Marvin's pulled it off with 'Surprise'. It's a sensational number.

We did know when Gregg was cast that the new number had to contain a degree of pyrotechnics in dance which would permit the display of his extraordinary talent. He has one quality in common with all great artists which is that when they have performed and done something totally miraculous, you feel they are just about to begin. That their juices, their performing capability have only just been touched. You feel that when you watch Olivier in the theatre. Gregg has it as a dancer.

Any doubts we had about casting him concerned whether he could act. Richie has no great scenes, but one or two moments that are terribly important and the question was, could Gregg pull them off? Well, the answer is yes, he could and he does. Certainly, if I had the opportunity, I would have great joy in asking him to play a straight part in any film I was going to make.

He had difficulties on *A Chorus Line* because not only was he there in his own right but Jeffrey asked him to be assistant choreographer as well. So he faced the considerable problem of having to maintain camaraderie with 'the line' and also, when necessary, to exert the authority of his other function. I don't say he was always successful in maintaining the balance. On the whole, though, he won the day, through affection and through the profound respect he inspired by being just that bit ahead of all the other dancers.

As a black American, Gregg has a marvelously positive attitude. He and I had a wonderful rapport. I personally believe that racial prejudice is so totally idiotic, so utterly assinine, that it should be brought into the open, placed in full view and ridiculed. The decision to do this, unspoken on Gregg's part and mine, resulted in a special affinity I had for him. I think, I hope that those around us were influenced by our special friendship.

Michael Douglas

ZACH

TV Debut
The Experiment

Off-Broadway
City Scene
Pinkville

Films
Debut
Hail Hero

Roles
Adam at 6 a.m., Summertree
Napoleon and Samantha, Coma
The China Syndrome, Running
It's My Turn, Star Chamber
Romancing the Stone

Co-Produced
One Flew Over the Cuckoo's Nest

Produced
The China Syndrome
Romancing the Stone

Television
The FBI
Medical Center
When Michael Calls
Streets of San Francisco

*U*ntil I stopped them, the cast called me 'Mr Douglas'.

It made me wonder, 'Jesus, how long have I been in this business?' For the first time in my life I had this feeling of being older. From another generation. I mean, *I* was always the younger generation.

My part was not one that allowed for being close to the rest of the company, although I was very fond of them all and we got along well. I talked to Richard early on and my suggestion was that distance would be a benefit. Other than being friendly, obviously, I wouldn't go out of my way to embrace the cast. It wasn't to do with status. It had to do with Zach, with maintaining his distance, emotionally, professionally and physically, from 'the line'.

A lot of the parts I've played were either sensitive young men or people full of idealism. And the truth of the matter is that actors often have most success playing villains. My father did a picture called *Champion* which turned his career around. And although Zach is not a villain, I was attracted to playing a man who put art before life, whose work was more important than his daily existence. Then, through the return of somebody who has been important to him, he begins to have an awareness of what exactly he's been missing. I love the single mindedness of Zach. And, with all that sensitivity being shown on the stage, I like his insensitivity. He has a tunnel vision and sees only what he is trying to get, rather than what it means to any other individual.

My mother and father got divorced when I was five and a half. I moved to New York City with my mother, who's a Bermudian, and she started living with a guy whom she married when I was twelve.

I certainly have a lot of respect for Kirk – we spent summers together – and we're quite close. But, as my father, he is the first to be forever grateful to Bill Darrid for the responsibility he assumed towards me when he married my mother. I find myself toasting step parents everywhere since there's a dearth of stories about men and women who have taken on their spouse's children from other marriages. They do it out of love and make the best job of it they can and maybe a bond with the kids does occur. So I do tend to remind people that I have a mother and stepfather who played a large part in rearing me. Both of them are involved in the theater and that's why *A Chorus Line* was the ultimate thrill: going back to New York, and doing a play and a movie rolled into one.

I knew Jeffrey Hornaday from *Romancing the Stone*. He came to Mexico to give Kathleen Turner and me some Latin dance steps for a scene which ultimately became just a short moment in the movie.

Jeffrey strikes me as a lot like myself. He's kind and diplomatic and very professional. Yet there's something else going on underneath. I think it's anger or frustration. I've had a lot of frustration in producing films. And one develops a strong revenge motive for all the people who've rejected your projects for a long time. You think, 'Someday I'm going to get there. I'm

going to get that picture made. I'm going to show that person.' A lot of times ambition comes from some form of anger. I got a kick out of Jeffrey. His talent is real and it's raw, too. What's so exciting is that it's built on instinct. His style of dancing is angry, almost primal. I think it's going to be a big plus for the movie.

Another thing that gave me a kick was watching the performers who had never been with a camera before. They hadn't had time to be intimidated. They were just joyful about the whole experience without any sense of the repercussions, of what it all might mean. That joy was due to the atmosphere Jeffrey and Richard created.

Richard likes to make movies the way I do. You create an environment that's as comfortable as possible on the assumption that you've hired people who all want to work very hard. Richard is not looking to create friction in the mistaken belief that the work will be better. One of the reasons I accepted the movie was because I admired his other musical, *Oh! What a Lovely War*, so much. But as an actor, I held him in awe, particularly for *Seance on a Wet Afternoon*.

As a director, he never imposed that ability other than when he'd simply illustrate a point by acting something out. I'd say, 'Don't you want to get back to it? I mean, you're so good.' And he'd just laugh. He's enormously supportive and one of his greatest strengths is that he has a very clear vision of the project, a through line, from which he never deviates. He's a joy in that, unlike some directors, he likes actors. I think some of the younger performers won't realise just how kind and supportive he is until they get offered other gigs. Another extraordinary quality which constantly amazed me was how he always appeared to have a moment for everyone, a moment of undivided concentration and attention. That's a wonderful quality to have, and also very smart. With Richard, because he is so busy, you have to get your thoughts together, to formulate your questions in a precise way. So he's got very good organisational skills. And he is a very secure man who can surround himself with the best people without ever feeling intimidated.

He has a good instinct about talent. Some of the people in the movie he really went to bat for ... I think he was absolutely right.

When he brought me to meet the company for the first time, they'd been rehearsing for a while and however shy they were, I was shy too. I remember saying hello to each of them and it was all a bit of a blur. But Alyson, who plays Cassie, took the trouble to come up afterwards and, out of the blue, gave me a hug and a kiss on the cheek. And I thought she had a giggle, a giggle in her belly and a sort of mischievous, rascal quality, like she had a secret. It's a nice quality, warm and friendly.

Then, later, I went to one of the dance rehearsals, and, not having been around dancers much, I found it a very exciting experience. I had to cross my legs a couple of times, try to be *blasé* about it. But, Jesus, the place reeked of energy, the physical energy of sex. It was very, very sexy.

I saw Alyson, and if she wasn't kicking her legs up to her ears, she'd be bending and stretching. And I thought, 'This part's looking better and better.' I enjoyed flirting with her. She was fun.

I loved her little beauty mark. I remember that and her unique style of cocking her head. Her sexiness, if I can equate it with Kathleen Turner's, is that both have a directness which is refreshing after all those coquettish dead ends. Both can look a guy straight in the eye, laugh with him and make him feel comfortable. With Alyson, you get the impression that she likes men, rather than feeling threatened or angry. And that combined with what I call 'having a secret' is what makes her sexy. The two most attractive qualities in a woman are a sense of humor and intelligence. And they usually go together.

I first saw Michael in *The China Syndrome* which, of course, he had also produced. I thought it a fascinating film which presented him with an opportunity to display a character of real intellect. So when Marti Baum rang me to say that Michael might be interested in playing Zach, I was prepared to throw my cap over the moon.

We, that is Cy, Ernie, Arnold and I, had been thrashing around for the right personality to play this very difficult character, who had been almost totally undefined in the show. Until that day we had no sense of having the ideal person in focus. Our initial thought, as with the rest of the cast, had been to find a new face, someone with no previous connotations. But, with one possible exception, we had failed.

Marti's call was, therefore, something of a god-send. The proffered terms under which Michael was prepared to accept the part are indicative of the man. He must now command a vast salary for any movie in which he appears and yet he was content to accept the relatively miniscule amount in our budget without any attempt to better it.

He also said that, since this was very much an ensemble production and the story really belonged to 'the chorus line', he did not wish for any kind of star billing and would prefer his name to appear alphabetically amongst the nineteen other featured players.

He was a joy to work with, always there, ready, word perfect and happy to play lines off – those spoken from behind the camera to cue other players actually

being filmed. He never looked for any special treatment or displayed any unacceptable flamboyance which might well have been expected, and indeed justified, from the man who produced *One Flew Over the Cuckoo's Nest* and had so recently scored a phenomenal success with *Romancing the Stone*.

The kids, of both sexes, adored him. And Michael is marvelous in the film, simply marvelous. Zach is a very difficult character to play without being over-abrasive and unsuitably bombastic. Michael does it superbly in a performance that is full of invention, integrity, charm and intelligence. I only hope that it will add further lustre to what is already a most distinguished career on both sides of the camera.

Cameron English

PAUL

Music Video
Captain EO and the Space Knights with Michael Jackson

Television
Fame (series regular), MGM

TV Variety Shows
The Tonight Show, Gypsy Roads, American Movie Awards, Star Search,
34th Emmy Awards, *Tribute to Martin Luther King, Star Salute to the
Olympics,* Macy's Thanksgiving Day Parade, *Kids from Fame* World
Tour, *Kids from Fame* Special

Special Skills
Football, singing, swimming, dancing, choreography, music

It doesn't embarrass me personally. But I guess it will be shocking to some people. I look on Paul and what he says and what he does as merely a part that I'm playing.

He comes from certain circumstances which make him have certain feelings. I think Paul is very brave because he makes himself go out and tell his story. He just says, 'Here I am. This is me. This is the way I talk and the way I dress.'

Paul's a very honest person.

We came to the scene with the very long speech at the end of the day. My mind kept blocking, just not connecting. I would have it focused on the lines and then I would think about what Richard had said, his directions, and try to put the two together. But on the evening it just didn't work.

I felt real comfortable with Richard, and the crew is the crew. I didn't feel like anybody disliked what I was doing. I was there to say what I had to say and I just took it moment by moment. That's the way I am.

My first job as a dancer was with the San Diego Ballet. I'd just turned seventeen and I was dancing professionally, getting a hundred dollars a week. Enough to get by. It wasn't great but I was just starting out and they let me be an apprentice in their company. So I had a really good opportunity to train and earn some money.

I was in *Fame* for three years and I never said a word. There were fifteen of us who were always there, dancing in the show every week and we worked really hard. It was like we'd dance and go home. When I toured England with *The Kids from Fame* we got a lot of feedback from the general public and it was nice that someone remembered us.

But, staying with the show, I could see my future as a dead end. I had to do something else. I had to take another step or just resign myself to the way it was. I wasn't happy. I wanted to reach out for other things.

I read about the Los Angeles open call for *A Chorus Line* in a trade paper and had about ten call-backs, mostly for dance. I read for Richard three times. All this over a period of about two months. Then a casting person in LA called me up and told me to start packing my bags. I'd got the job.

That's still just so amazing to me. Friends come up to me and say, 'God, you're really lucky because so many thousands auditioned.'

At the time I wasn't thinking about pressure . . . I was just one person in a bunch. Actually getting the part is what I'll remember the most.

Richard was a really interesting teacher because I hadn't had any acting experience before we shot *A Chorus Line*. He's very intimate and personal with feelings. And it's nice when a professional talks to you like that. I've just had it with situations where you just go in and do your stuff and that's it. He works *with* you and I felt like, 'Wow, this big guy is talking to *me*.' It's neat. Richard is really honest and I believed everything he said. That made me want to work for him, to produce something for him. It's not like he was trying to contrive something out of me. He was confirming what I did and he believed in me. That made me want to give more and support him. So it was a mutual relationship which felt very nice.

I hope this movie will get me a foot in the door to doing some more serious acting. I don't want to do that leading-man type nothing part that any handsome person can do. I want to do things that stretch me a lot in different ways. Right now it's going really good and I'm flowing with all the positive energies. But I'm not going to count my chickens before they hatch. I have an agent now. And, after the movie, my *resumé* looks better.

I'm a professional dancer but I don't think of myself as a gypsy. That's because I had the security of working on *Fame*. Gypsies are always wandering around, always on the move, going to different locations where the work is. It's very short term. Everything's month to month. Living out of a suitcase.

Like Paul, my character in the movie, I started dancing very late. I began with ballet and then went on to jazz, tap, modern, mostly everything. It was something to do, athletic wise, and it made me feel comfortable. It was a way of expressing myself but I didn't have to talk. Now I do want to talk.

★ ★ ★

We were very tempted to cast Sammy Williams who created Paul in the show and indeed won a Tony for his performance. And, of course, we tested him. But, believing very much that, if the film was to work, it had to be of today and truly concerned with young people facing the dilemmas and problems that their age group's cruelly disproportionate unemployment poses throughout the world, it seemed wrong to introduce someone who was eight or ten years older than most of 'the line'.

So I decided to play Cameron.

He was certainly satisfactory as far as dance was concerned, but his acting experience was negligible. So it was a great gamble. But one, I think, that's come off very well.

He has a difficult piece of acting to do, in that, to all intents and purposes, he is faced with a monologue. Feeling very much for him as an actor, I knew that the ability to maintain and play a speech which runs for several minutes was only part of the problem.

More importantly, having started on that speech, he had to be so susceptible to the emotions he was recalling that they would become evident. And the scene doesn't work unless, in the latter part, there's a long uninterrupted flow. It was very touching that the whole crew obviously cared as much about that scene as Cameron and I did. On the evening that we came to it, for various reasons, we never actually reached concert pitch although we went on a bit beyond the normal day. The crew was crossing fingers, crossing everything in sight, willing Cameron to pull it off. But ultimately he and I decided, although we had gone into penalty in the ·expectation of finishing, that we'd have to try again the following day.

As we broke and everyone prepared to go home, the unit shop steward came over and said that the boys had had a little meeting. If we'd got the scene, they would have put in for overtime, but as we hadn't they'd agreed to waive it.

This gesture was indicative of the atmosphere throughout the production. The kids endeared themselves to the crew enormously because, for most of them, it was their first big break and they didn't indulge in histrionics or silly temperaments and the technicians admired that very much, adored them and wanted them all to succeed.

Tony Fields

AL

Films
Protocol, Columbia Pictures
Night Shift, The Ladd Company

Television
Solid Gold
Academy Awards 1984, ABC
John Davidson Christmas Special
Bobby Vinton's Rock-'n-Rollers
L'il Abner's Dogpatch Today (Pilot)

Music Videos
Beat It, with Michael Jackson
Thriller, with Michael Jackson
Running with the Night, with Lionel Richie
Perfect, with Jermaine Jackson

Theater
Debbie Reynold's Nightclub Act, National/International Tour
George M!
The Music Man
Bye Bye Birdie
Godspell
Pepper Street

Special Skills
Martial arts, tumbling, trampoline, horseback riding, motorcycle

*A*t the open cattle call in Los Angeles there were hundreds of people. Literally hundreds. That was the start of my experience of getting the role. It was one of the hardest things I've ever done. I wanted it so bad, it was frightening.

Finally I was told I would be flown to New York to screen test. That's when the nerves really set in. There, I met Nicole Fosse who plays my wife. Ernie Martin had said at one of the auditions, 'I'd like to get you and Gwen Verdon and Bob Fosse's daughter because she's a petite blonde and, compared with most dancers, you're a giant. The two of you would be like Fay Wray and King Kong.'

We hit it off right away. The chemistry just clicked. As I went in for my screen test another guy who was up for Al was just leaving. They had tried to work it out so that we didn't see each other. But we came face to face. After the screen test there was no reaction except, 'Thank you very much.' That's the killer, when they're so cool . . .

So, weeks went by and I ate like a pig, something I was never able to do in all the years I was on TV in *Solid Gold*. Always had to watch the waistline for fear of the Spandex blimp. I never wanted to leave home because I didn't want to have the machine pick up *the* call if it came. All the confidence I had built up previously, saying when I put my mind to something I get it because I work hard and I love it . . . all that had been annihilated. I even forgot I had ever thought that way. I had been made so humble, a hermit. I was like, 'Please choose, use me, choose me. Oh God, I need this job.'

Finally, I bought this key chain with an imitation *Chorus Line* ticket on it dated Wednesday, 21 April. And I said, this is going to be good luck. Either I'll hear on a Wednesday or on the twenty-first. So I woke up on Saturday, April 21, and I'll never forget that I looked at the clock and it was ten twenty-one. And the phone rang.

It was long distance. 'Tony, this is Ernie Martin. You got the job.'

The main lesson I learned is that you must always be humble and you must always have that doubt. When everything is going great and you think you're so big, go stand on the seashore and look out at the ocean and know how small you are.

So, all of a sudden, I am in New York and every person – Richard Attenborough, Jeffrey Hornaday, people on the crew, people in the street, my trainer, the lady I rent my apartment from – all of a sudden these people believe in Tony Fields. Until then only I believed in me. From childhood, just doing it myself. There was never support. Never anybody to say, 'Go, go, go.' There was just me. Never knowing if I really had it.

Then I start working with Richard, after coming from the stage where everything is big, and all of a sudden I'm told to do absolutely nothing.

Richard said, 'Just think, my heart, and it will come across.'

All those times of growing up and people telling me I'm such a thoughtless person, so selfish, and this man suddenly takes me and totally puts his hands around me, just like closes in everything and says, 'Just forget and think. Look at yourself. You're beautiful.'

And then I saw the result on the screen and I cried. I sat there and my eyes filled up with tears because it was so real and so right. No one wants to be put on display unless they're a raving beauty – which God knows, I'm not. What Richard did for me was to give me this incredible self-esteem. So I could look at myself for the first time and say, 'You really are good. You're a nice person.'

Jeffrey Hornaday and I became very good friends. To me he's a genius. Here is this twenty-seven-year-old choreographer who does so much more than just teach you a step. I mean I've worked with choreographers who make people literally cry. They say the most excruciating things to get the most from dancers. Jeffrey never had to ask us to get up off our butts to learn something. People were standing there waiting. Like, where's the next step?

The team of Attenborough and Hornaday is really incredible. Everybody had assumed that Richard would go with an older choreographer. Yet he went with this young, energetic guy and they make a team of trust, realism and honesty. The man in his sixties and the man in his twenties … they are one and the same. Jeffrey sat at Richard's side and hung on his every word. He was like a *guru* to Jeffrey.

But, at the same time, Richard was as youthful as we were and willing to learn from us. 'And the students

shall teach the teacher…' I can't quote exactly but that's how it was.

★ ★ ★

One of the difficulties of dealing with group performance is that you've got to allow every player, during lining up or rehearsal – off screen as it were – to exert their own personality. Tony is the extrovert of all time and, for his own satisfaction, has to be the life and soul of the party. One had to permit him to display that aspect of his psyche, although at times it could disrupt other people's attention. On the other hand, one has to say that whenever things got a bit tough or tedious, he could always be counted on to lift the atmosphere.

Despite the immense skills, now properly recognised, of casting directors, the final choice is, or should be, the director's. There are two forms of casting. In one, as with Jan Gan Boyd, you wish ultimately to reveal aspects of character and personality which are not evident at first sight. Alternatively, there is casting in which the character's impact, from the second he or she arrives on the screen, is instantly and totally defined.

The conventional casting of Al would have been to choose a fairly average, good-looking guy. I wanted something different.

There were some wonderful auditions, but none of the other actors registered with the same degree of screen personality as Tony. He has immense character. And, if you saw him walking down the street, he's the last person on earth you'd suspect was a dancer. He's the absolute antithesis; heavily muscled with a huge, broad chest. He could be a football player. It was interesting, having settled for this external impact, that one was slowly able to discover certain vulnerabilities within which made the character of Al, when he talked about his talent, extremely touching. His huge animal-like cossetting of his little wife, Kristine, was, even in the tests, very moving.

I therefore fought very hard for Tony. It wasn't easy. There was considerable opposition because people felt it was way-out casting. But, having seen the final movie, I am quite sure the decision was a correct one. His Al, which in other hands might have been somewhat cardboard, is a truly three-dimensional character.

Nicole Fosse

KRISTINE

Film
Call Backs (Wendy), CTC Films

Television
How to Be a Man, CBS
Out of Step, ABC

Music Video
Hang Up the Phone, with Annie Golden

Dinner Theater
Can Can, with Yvonne deCarlo

Concert Dance
Cleveland Ballet, 2 years, apprentice

My father said, 'I'm going to try and teach you everything I know about acting. Everything I've learned in fifty-eight years, I'm going to try and teach you in six hours. Okay?'

This was when I kept getting called back for the movie. I wanted to give it the best shot I possibly could so I went to him with my scenes and said, 'Help.'

Before playing Kristine, I'd only had one line in a movie, *All That Jazz*. But that was nepotism because it was my father's movie. So it doesn't really count.

Kristine is very young, very nervous. Her nerves get in the way of her being able to function. I don't think she's dumb. The night before an audition she sits at home and rehearses what she's going to say about herself. But when the time comes, she is so overwhelmed her mind's a total blank.

I remember a couple of times my father had me do the entire scene where Kristine tries to speak while I was tying up my shoelace, just to give me something else to think about. Then he'd ask me a question and I'd forget what I was supposed to say. So I learned a lot just getting the job on *A Chorus Line*.

I'd been working with an actor I already knew through my parents who was up for the part of Al, Kristine's husband. He was in a play at the time and I'd go over to his dressing room and we'd rehearse our scene together. We did this a couple of times a week over a long period and just sit around, talking and getting to know each other. We tried to develop a husband and wife kind of relationship.

We went in one morning – the day before the screen test – for a rehearsal with Sir Richard. Then after we'd both left the room, they called me in again and asked if I would mind going back at the end of the day. They had somebody else coming for Al. I felt faithful to the actor I already knew. He is a really nice person. So when I met Tony Fields, my first reaction was stand-offish. I didn't know Tony, which isn't to say I didn't like him. I just didn't know him. I liked the other guy.

And then when we screen-tested, Tony was so sweet. Here was this big guy, big, tough guy, and he'd look at me with these soft, warm cow eyes and I thought, 'Wow! This is great. This is perfect.'

Before, I had been with the Cleveland Ballet as an apprentice and I'd frayed my Achilles tendon and couldn't dance at all. I tried and it just didn't work, only made it worse. It was very depressing to sit around and watch everybody else rehearsing *Swan Lake*. I mean it's the epitome of ballet to run around and be a swan. I couldn't stand it. I knew that I was going to be emotionally disturbed if I had to sit in Cleveland for three weeks so I decided to go back to New York. When I got there I called my agent and he said, 'How about you go on this interview for the *Chorus Line* movie?'

So I went and was interviewed by the casting agency. Cy Feuer, who was sitting there, asked if I sang. I told him that I didn't really sing but I could carry a tune. Then he asked if I'd kept up with my jazz.

And I said, 'Yes.' Which was a lie because I'd been doing ballet all along.

I'm an only child so I don't know exactly, but I would assume that my experience on the movie was similar to having a big family. You like some of your brothers and sisters and some you don't. You get along great and then you turn around and fight.

In the beginning, during the rehearsal period, I noticed a lot of hype, a lot of energy. There was all this pulling and tugging for Sir Richard or Jeffrey's attention, as if people were saying the whole time, 'Look at me, look at me . . . '

That really did bother me for a while because I've never liked to get involved in that kind of thing. Then you feel nobody's noticing you, so you try doing it too. And you can't. So you say to yourself, 'What am I doing? Forget it. Just do your job. When they say, "Kick," kick, when they say "Talk," talk . . . and do it as well as you can.' But that didn't last long. It was just in the rehearsal period.

Although I was brought up in show business, I still don't know if I want to be in it. There is so much out there that I'd be interested in trying. Being in the movie was fun. It was great. But I don't want to spend the whole of my life on a stage or on a film set kicking my legs and belting it out.

★ ★ ★

There was a very real danger that Kristine could become a caricature. The casting, therefore, was very delicate and had to be seen in concert with that of Al. I believed that the only way one could overcome the problem of caricature was to have the scene in which Kristine speaks to Zach played with absolute truth. If we engaged an actress who, for one moment, lost the reality of what she was doing, the sincerity, then the character would fly out of the window. There was no possible way of retrieving it. The moment was so brief.

Therefore, I was looking for a personality who could embody all Kristine's awkwardness and gaucheness in her performance, yet was graceful enough to be acceptable as a ballet dancer and equally capable of presenting this scatterbrain.

There were a number of possibilities for the part of Kristine and a lot of debate, but I have to say that, right from the very beginning, I felt overwhelmingly we should choose Nicole.

I had no idea of her background when I first selected her for a screen test and it was only when we came to film it that Cy Feuer said to me, 'Do you know that's Gwen Verdon and Bob Fosse's daughter?' I didn't, but both her parents have been heroes of mine for some time. Bob is not only a brilliant choreographer but also a marvelous director and Gwen won my heart as the queen of Broadway musicals. She came to visit Nicole, and it was a great joy to meet her *(see below)*.

Nicole worked terribly hard as an actress. She examined every single moment involving Kristine to discover what her character's reactions would be. And if she wasn't sure, then over she'd come with her innocent eyes displaying her anxieties and concerns, and ask me if she was correct.

If she wants to – and I don't think she yet knows – I am sure she could have a career as an actress. She obviously has a future as a dancer.

Vicki Frederick

SHEILA

Broadway
Minnie's Boys (Chorus)
Cyrano (Chorus)
The Rothschilds (Chorus)
Pippin
Dancin' – New York Outer Critics Award
Los Angeles Critics Circle Award
A Chorus Line (Cassie), also Los Angeles Company

Television
Happy Days
Laverne and Shirley
Mork and Mindy

Films
All the Marbles, with Peter Falk
Stick, with Burt Reynolds
All That Jazz

It was so strange. In 1974 there were all these stories going around about people giving taped interviews and they were going into a workshop with Michael Bennett. And I knew those people, the people that *A Chorus Line* is about. I was on Broadway at the time, in Bob Fosse's *Pippin*. I knew Cassie and her story. I knew the girl who was really Sheila, my part in the movie. The girl whose story was 'Tits and Ass' wasn't cast originally but she's played Val on Broadway since. And she did have a little breast enlargement and maybe her nose done. But she didn't have her bum pulled up.

A lot of these people weren't in the show when it opened. Then, over the years, slowly but surely, they did get to play themselves.

When this little show at the Public Theater first happened, you couldn't get in to see it. At that time going down to the East Village, for New Yorkers, was like taking your life in your hands. I mean, where was the East Village? Well, people did go there and you couldn't get near the theater because of the limousines. Gene Kelly, Fred Astaire … they were all there. And they were all crying.

A Chorus Line is about people. You don't have to be a dancer to understand it. It's about all the hopes and dreams that everybody has somewhere along the line. The chorus dancers were a sort of enigma. They always kicked and they were very pretty. Although not many people ever realised it, they worked hard too. Somebody decided to find out what made them tick.

That, to me, is the essence of the story. Why do they want to get up on stage and do the same thing for eight shows a week? Behind the star, for no recognition and for very little money?

My first audition on Broadway was for *Zorba*. It was an open call – what we call a 'cattle call'. I was seventeen, I guess, and there had to be about a hundred and fifty girls, all in black leotards, black tights and very high-heeled character shoes. And I stood out. I came in my pink ballet slippers and pink tights. Which you do not wear to a Broadway audition.

But I did get a call back. And, of course, I went directly from the theater and bought black tights and very high character shoes. When I got right down to the end, to the finals, I thought, 'This is a snap, I'm going to get this job.' And right at the very last minute, I was cut.

What I discovered that day was that you really have to believe in yourself. Your talent is something that is innate only in you. You must always nurture that. All of us, in this profession, are very fragile. Everybody deals with rejection in a different way. If you can't handle it, then you're going to ruin yourself and your talent. Because that's what this business is about: rejection. You just have to go in and be judged, over and over again. Lay yourself on the line.

My first real shot at acting was when Michael Bennett gave me Cassie, on Broadway. Initially, when I first saw the show, I thought I would be right for Sheila. Because of the things that had gone on in my life, coming from a family where the marriage wasn't that good, I identified a lot. But Michael wanted me to do Cassie. I think because I was so quiet and angelic looking. He didn't know me at the time, however!

When it came to the movie, I wanted Sheila so badly. Because I thought it was a real opportunity to work on a character that I felt strongly about and also to work with Sir Richard Attenborough. I was very frightened of him at first. I thought, 'Oh, my God, supposing he asks about Shakespeare? I don't know any Shakespeare.' It was very intimidating. Usually I audition very badly. Except, I think, with this movie. I felt that Richard knew I could do it. And the previous work he'd done as an actor, that was very important to me. He's a snake charmer, anyway. He makes you feel you can do anything. If he told me I could pilot Concorde across the Atlantic, I'd say, 'Sure, of course I can.'

I've been very fortunate on Broadway. I've worked with some of the best. But to work with a director of Richard's stature, in film, I was thrilled.

This is like my fourth or fifth movie. And I'm still waiting for the glamor. That isn't what it's all about. The good part of it is working on a character, trying to find out what it is, and the collaboration between you and the director.

When I came back to New York for dance rehearsals in August 1984, I had already been working for two months with a trainer. Oh, yes, I knew. I knew. When I saw Mr Hornaday's choreography, I said, 'Vicky, what have you gotten yourself into? You're going to be on crutches.' And, of course, I was cracking

jokes left and right because I was scared to death to find myself in this group of eighteen- and twenty-year-olds. Even though I'd run and hiked with the trainer for like three and four hours a day to get back into shape. I thought, 'Lord, how am I going to get these thighs up and down that fast?'

Basically, Sheila started dancing because it was an escape. She puts on a great act, cracking the one-liners, but that's just a cover up. She's insecure and scared to death. She would very much like to have accomplished more but was always afraid to ask for too much.

Personally, I've always said I want it all. And I think everybody can have it … but only to a certain degree. When I was pregnant with my daughter, Amanda, I was doing *A Chorus Line*, dancing in the show, until my fifth month. When she was born, I suddenly became this domestic person. Before, I used to go to Bloomingdales and have anxiety attacks when it came to picking out kitchen curtains. And then I had my daughter and that's all I wanted to do. I didn't want to know about show business. I didn't want to know about dancing. I just wanted to be with my baby.

Amanda was in New York with me for a good part of the months we were making the movie. But there would be periods when I would be rehearsing and shooting and not able to spend time with her, and she'd fly to Los Angeles where my husband was working. So she became a bi-coastal baby at twenty-six months. And that's real hard.

I would be guilty because I was working and would think, 'Oh, my God, I ought to be home with my baby.' Then I would be home, having a wonderful time with Amanda, and, in the back of my head, would be guilty because I should have been working on my part.

When we'd nearly finished the movie, the other kids would be sitting around discussing their next project, what was coming up. The irons in the fire, as they say. At one time, I used to be like that. And now what I wanted was to go home and be Mommy. I knew also that I'd be thrilled doing that for six weeks, then I'd get a little itchy, wanting to read scripts. But whatever work I do in the next two or three years, it will be done in LA. You do have to compromise. Before *A Chorus Line* I thought, 'No, you don't.' But you do. You do.

★ ★ ★

Ultimately, there remained two real contenders for the part of Sheila, and we tested them both extensively. In the end I cast Vicki not only because she fitted more comfortably into 'the line' but also because she had a particular quality which I sought for Sheila. She had the talent to play a very show-business character with theatrical pay-off lines and yet, at the same time, invest Sheila with a stamp of truth.

Of all the characters in the show, it struck me that Sheila was the most susceptible to caricature. In the theatre everything is of necessity drawn with broad strokes, whereas on film it was vital that the performance be couched in absolutely real terms.

Quite apart from her marvelous performance, I am indebted to Vicki for other reasons. She was, by a few years, the oldest member of the cast actually on 'the line'. Consequently, by virtue not only of seniority but also because of her stature in the business, she became 'den mother' to the younger members of the cast. Whenever there was the possibility of a breakdown of discipline or lack of concentration, it was always Vicki, behind the scenes, who pulled everybody back into shape. I do know that on one or two occasions several of the kids felt the whip of her tongue in reaction to their sometimes unthinking adolescent behavior.

It was an extraordinary experience, living as a group – the dancers, Jeffrey and me – for over seven months. Once we moved from the rehearsal studio into the Mark Hellinger Theater, the kids paired up to share dressing rooms. And in a way it was like running a boarding school. Their interaction was a necessary way of maintaining adrenalin. But creating the balance between permitting idiotic pranks and conforming to the strict disciplines which are an integral part of a dancer's existence was very delicate. In no small measure, Vicki helped maintain that correct proportion.

What Vicki brings to the screen, having started her career essentially in the theater, is exceptional, I think. She's a smashing actress. Her moments in 'At the Ballet' and in a scene she has at the end of the movie are exquisitely played with an additional stratum of vulnerability which, for me, makes Sheila into a truly three-dimensional character and a very touching one.

Michelle Johnston

BEBE

Television
Rock Palace (dancer/guest host), NBC
T.J. Hooker
Mama's Family
Emmy Awards (dancer)

Films
Staying Alive
One from the Heart

Community Theater
Grease, Peter Pan, The Boyfriend, Alice in Wonderland

Stage
Act III Dancers (choreographer), Yuzawa, Japan
Juraku World Show (lead dancer), Iizaka, Japan

In my break from rehearsal I went to the open call. I nearly left when I saw there were about five million people outside. I only had an hour. But, luckily for me, as it turned out, I went right up to the person on the door and said, 'Look, I'm in a show for NBC right down the street. Do you think I could just sneak in there, real quick?'

So she stuck me in like the next group and I didn't even know the choreography. I stood at the side trying to pick it up as fast as I could and then I jumped in there, thinking I'd be cut immediately. Fifteen minutes later a small group of us did it again and they kept me. And I said, 'Look, I've got to go to rehearsal. How long is this going to last?'

They said that Jeffrey liked me a lot . . . so could I stick around for a couple of hours. I called my rehearsal and they said I could stay. Well, I kept getting called back and about thirty of us were asked to rehearse once a week. And I kept thinking I would never get it because I couldn't act and I couldn't sing and I didn't even know what part I was up for. Then Richard came to LA and they announced they'd call out our names and the characters. And they said Bebe for me.

In the movie Bebe Benson is nineteen years old. She has always had an inferiority complex and a problem dealing with herself physically and mentally. She is just trying to accept herself, accept what she is. She's not a raving beauty and never will be but there is something about her, something very talented and intense.

My mother never said that I was ugly or anything. She always thought I was like Bebe. I was very unique, and 'Well, you'll never be a classic beauty, Michelle, you don't have the facial structure or anything. You're just very unique looking. That'll work because you have talent and that's all that matters.'

But, as an adolescent, you don't want to hear that, you know? I didn't want to hear that I was different, exotic and talented. I just wanted to be all-American and cute.

Up to eleven or twelve years old, I was extremely popular in school. Then I started going through my adolescence. My face started breaking out and I had the strangest hair. It used to be long, straight and blonde. Slowly it started frizzing up around the temples and then it started falling out. I was so blonde. I had blonde eyebrows and eyelashes and I never wore any make-up. I was very odd looking, very strange. In California you were supposed to have that typical look. And I just didn't qualify.

People at school used to say terrible, terrible things and call me horrible names. I used to be teased because of my acne and everything. It was devastating, the worst two years of my life, from twelve to fourteen years old. There were times when I wanted to cry so bad I would just run out of the classroom and into the bathroom to be alone.

But I'm glad now. I wouldn't really want to change anything. If it had been easier for me in school, I wouldn't have pushed so hard in my career. It wouldn't have been that important to me. Dancing was the only thing that I had to hold onto, the only thing that kept me sane because I loved it so much and I knew when I went to my classes everything *was* beautiful at the ballet. It felt so good and I was the best person in the class. That's the only time I received real praise from anybody.

By the time I was fifteen my face was clearing up a bit and my hair was looking more normal and I started wearing mascara. Still not a beauty, by any means, but a little more presentable. And I'd learned to use humor, always being the class clown. So they would think, 'Yes, she's fun to be around. She's cool. She's not cute but she's real funny.' It's so sad. At that age you'd do anything to be popular, anything to be accepted.

Then, when I was sixteen, I totally rebelled and went in the opposite direction. I started dressing real strange for school. Long before they were anything near in style, I used to wear see-through plastic pants with my dance clothes underneath and dark sunglasses and hats.

I would hang out with my friend, Kelly. We won a ballet scholarship together and our teacher gave us this strict diet and told us our perfect weight which was just ridiculously low. I mean, really insane. Because I'd always had approval from my dance teachers, I wanted to please her. I couldn't even think if I liked my own body any more. If she didn't like it, then she was right. I trusted her. She was like a god to me. But Kelly and I wanted some control over our lives.

So all we did in class was talk about what would we buy to eat afterwards and where could we throw up.

At your house? No, we can't at my house. Maybe in the back yard, into a paper bag. That's what we'll have to do. It was just so gross.

We would do that like every day. Three times a day. It seemed like a kind of cool thing to do. We used to read books about how ballet dancers did it. I wanted to be a *prima ballerina*, so I had to do it too. It ruled our lives for about a year. It was just a waste. Waste of a year.

We thought we could get something over on the teacher. Because I kept it a little more under control, she never found out with me. She found out with Kelly, who ended up being hospitalised. They had like tubes going up her nose. Oh, it was horrible.

Once I started working in films, I stopped doing it really. But it was difficult for me in New York during *Chorus Line* because I didn't have a boyfriend. The first time since I was fifteen. I think I work better when I'm with somebody. It makes me feel relaxed and secure.

For dancers, it's hard to be with anyone who isn't in the business because they are the only ones who understand. There's that creativity, that energy you don't find in an accountant. Most of my show business friends are gay or bisexual. I have very few male friends who are straight. Which is kind of unfortunate. But it makes for good friendships. You don't have to worry that there's going to be a problem if you want a platonic relationship. And they give you really good advice. Because they can see from both sides. I think straight people usually have more hang-ups than gay ones. I don't know why.

I had friends in high school who would never admit they were gay, but they told me and we would talk about it. It didn't make any difference. They were just who they were. And they helped me because they understood. Gay men know about having to keep the weight down because they are just as meticulous as women about their looks. They have the sensitivity of women, they are more caring. I think it frightens straight men, the problems I had, because they've never had to deal with that.

I don't think I've ever seen anybody dance quite like Michelle, and Jeffrey endorses the fact that technically she is exceptional. We brought her to New York for camera tests and there was no question. Michelle was a standout.

There are some actors and actresses who register in the theater and some who appear almost devoid of any special quality to the eye but create the most extraordinary impact in front of the camera. I understand Marilyn Monroe had that quality. I believe that Michelle shares it too.

Some time after the test we flew to Los Angeles to see the kids again and to talk to them about playing various parts. We had asked Michelle if she would come and meet us at the Beverly Hills Hotel.

Cy, Ernie, Arnold and I were coming out of the Polo Lounge and walking towards the house phones which are nearby. A girl was using one of them, with her back towards us. I took a terrible gamble because I didn't know her all that well, but I was sure it was Michelle. So I crept up behind, put my arms round her waist and whispered into her free ear, 'Hi, Bebe.'

She let out a piercing scream. The entire foyer of the hotel came to a standstill, with everyone convinced that there'd been an indecent assault. Which was pretty near the truth. She came upstairs with us and simply couldn't contain herself. She couldn't find words at all but kept on making noises, sort of expletives of disbelief.

In directing actors and actresses, there are those who require a lot of rehearsal and those who require next to none and there are those for whom rehearsal is almost always a disaster. And Michelle pretty well falls into the last category. Once she starts to think about what she's doing objectively, the performance flies out of the window. You've got to try and grab it the first time it's there. If you can, then she's magic.

I think she has a remarkable career ahead of her if she's properly nurtured. She's had a fairly wild life and, at one point towards the end of shooting, when perhaps she was a little lost and lonely, having no boyfriend in New York, the problem she'd had with bulimia re-emerged. It affected both her personality and her looks. Bless her, in my position of *loco parentis,* she turned to me for support. We talked about it extensively and, having been recommended to a specialist, she overcame it. She has tremendous strength of will. Correctly handled and well advised in career decisions, she has a terrific future.

Janet Jones

JUDY

Films
The Flamingo Kid (female lead)
Grease II
Staying Alive
The Beastmaster
Annie
One from the Heart

Television Series
Dance Fever

Television
Somewhere in Paradise
Charlie's Angels
Wheel of Fortune (co-host)

*H*e called me Ugly.

After my first couple of days on the movie, Sir Richard came up to me. 'You know, Janet, I've got the best ever nickname for you.'

A bit later, he was up in the balcony of the theater and I was down on the stage with a hundred and nineteen other dancers for the opening sequence. And from all the way up there, he yells, 'Hey, Ugly, move to the right.'

I'm happy that he gave me a nickname. It's a nice thing between us. A little later, I noticed he was wearing these pants. They were fine but it was like now he was with a group of kids who wore Levis a lot and they were the symbol of America's clothing. I told him what I thought and he kept teasing, 'Where are my blue jeans, then, Ugly?'

So I got him a pair of Levis and he wore them every day. Someone said, after a while, that he didn't have to hang them up. They'd just stand by themselves in the corner. But he did have them washed. They were done at the theater. For Christmas I bought him a pair of black ones. I like to see him in Levis. He looks good in them, even if they are a bit baggy.

I tell you, Sir Richard knows how to push the magic button. There's a moment in the movie when I have to burst out laughing. I was terrified of that. A month before, I'd laugh a lot on the set and joke around but as soon as they told me that scene was coming up, I became solemn and quiet and sat in a corner. I just did not think it was going to work.

I didn't know if 'the line', the other people on the stage, would bother me. Make me too intimidated. I knew I wouldn't be laughing at the dialog because it was stale. I'd rehearsed it so often. But, once I stepped out of that line and away from everybody, it was like a private world between Sir Richard and me. He did it. He made it work by giving me confidence.

I play Judy Munro, a girl who's very self-confident. She had a good childhood and she's more normal than anybody else at the audition even though she can be a little off the wall. She laughs a lot because she's having fun with the day, more so than a lot of pressure. She wants the job real bad but it's not going to kill her if she doesn't get it.

I started dancing late, at fifteen. Until then I wanted to be a professional softball player when I grew up. Honestly. I was thinking of the St Louis Hummers. I never had a girlfriend until I went to dance class.

I have six brothers and sisters and I'm from a town I lived in pretty much the whole of my life. I was a tomboy. I didn't even get asked out to the Prom. Then, one day, I was at an all-star baseball game and I was playing catcher and this girl I knew was batting. 'Gosh, I gotta leave early,' she says. 'I gotta go to my dance recital. Would you like to come later?'

So I went along and when I saw one girl dance by herself onstage that's when I said, 'Hey, that's what I want to do. That's going to be me.'

I started going to dance classes around three o'clock after school every day and stayed there until ten o'clock at night. That's what my family couldn't understand. Why I had to be there so long. They didn't have any dance knowledge at all and it was a struggle for me to get away from home every night.

Then I heard about the 'Miss Dance of America' pageant and entered just for fun. My father passed away about two months before I won the title 'Miss Dance of St Louis' when I was sixteen and a half. It was very traumatic.

I went on to win 'Miss Dance of Missouri'. That was a total shock to the whole community. Then there was the 'Miss Dance of America' pageant. Missouri had never won. In twenty-seven years, they had never won the competition. Well, I won. It was very, very exciting. All of a sudden, I was someone.

And since then, when I did *Dance Fever*, *The Flamingo Kid* and *A Chorus Line*, my family have been very proud of me. And high school friends are telling other high school friends, 'Do you believe Janet Jones? Do you believe what she's doing?'

★ ★ ★

Ugly desperately wanted to play in *Chorus Line*. She took part in all the major Los Angeles auditions and Jeffrey pronounced that even if she wasn't quite there at that moment, she could be an extraordinary dancer in terms of the choreography he had in mind. She had the most wonderful figure and presence and it was plain that, if she could fit into the mosaic that would make up 'the line', then she'd be a tremendous asset. The obvious and, in a way, the only part she could play was Judy.

Although she wanted at that particular time to be a model, and getting her name and face on the cover of some of the major American magazines was the height of her aspirations, she was essentially a dancer. However, I think she was also fascinated with acting.

She came to the Beverly Hills Hotel to meet Cy, Ernie, Arnold and me and I suggested she come into the bedroom while the others waited in the sitting-room so that I could work with her for half an hour and discover whether she could, in fact, act. (I suppose this must be one of the few occasions when an aspiring actress might say she won her part in the director's bedroom without blushing.)

Anyway, when we emerged I was convinced that if I could but engender the right circumstances on the set, she would perform very well as Judy. The point being that her principal moment comes when she has to burst into roars of laughter at a silly joke of her own. It's not an easy thing to do. You can attempt it technically or you can attempt it by motivation, or by a combination of the two. It seemed the only way Ugly was going to do it was if I could amuse and relax her sufficiently. Although we never achieved it in the hotel, there was sufficient to indicate she could do it under shooting conditions which are, in themselves, very daunting and tend to inhibit any actor or actress. We offered her Judy. We never tested her and, when the day came, she certainly did come up with it.

Pam Klinger

MAGGIE

Broadway & International
A Chorus Line (Maggie)

Regional Theater
The King and I (Princess)

Stock
Pittsburgh Civic Light Opera; *Bye Bye Birdie, Cabaret* (Telephone Girl),
The Red Mill, Funny Girl (Polly), *Good News, Camelot, My Fair Lady,*
No, No, Nanette, Paint Your Wagon, Naughty Marietta (Graziella),
Sweet Charity, Fanny.

Revue
Stairway to the Stars, Rainbow Room, NY

There was no question, ever, of faking it. I had to start back to camera and then turn so my face filled the screen while my eyes filled with tears. First of all, Sir Richard asked me what I needed to get that emotion going inside of me. Did I want a moment alone? I said I just wanted him to walk with me and hold my hand. And while we walked, he talked. I won't tell anyone exactly what he said but it wasn't specific words that helped me get my emotional prep. I needed to have him there because he made me feel secure. I idolise him. And, I don't know why ... he makes me cry.

Maggie, my character, is like the girl-next-door, very sweet and innocent. Sir Richard described her as almost like a Madonna, which I found very interesting. I kind of got goose bumps when he said that. She has a lot of pain inside and yet, I think, she is very strong. She's a survivor.

Maggie was born to keep her parents together and, when that failed, they didn't want her. What really makes me relate to Maggie is that I'm completely the opposite. My mother and father have given my sister and me everything. We got a car on our sixteenth birthday. They put us through college. But I don't think we're spoiled, because we'd do anything for them. I look at our family and I think, God, if I ever have kids I would do exactly what they did. They did it right.

As far as playing Maggie goes, I looked back at my childhood and wondered what it would have been like without them. That's how I related to her life. And it seemed to work.

I don't really know how it happened that both my younger sister, Cindi, and I both went into show-business. Homestead, where we come from, is a very, very small town. Neither my mother nor my father were in show business, but my father has a great tenor voice. I began singing lessons very early, at the age of ten. Thanks to my mother, I'd started dancing when I was two.

Although I'd been playing the part on Broadway for three years, I never thought I would get to play Maggie in the movie. Never, ever. Maggie's a Californian and I figured they'd choose a blonde and, if she couldn't sing, they could easily dub in another voice.

When I was doing the show, I knew Sir Richard was there a couple of times but, thank goodness, we didn't find out until the break. My number was over by then. One night, after the performance, he was waiting at the bottom of the stairs. He introduced himself and I was tongue-tied, of course. The next day my agent called and said I had an appointment to audition. I think every single person who ever played Maggie in the show was there. On Broadway and on tour. I saw at least eleven Maggies. Plus the original.

I think when I went back for the fourth time to dance for Sir Richard was when it really hit me. I'm mainly a singer, my strong point is singing, and dancing comes second. But after that dance audition and my first reading for him, I decided I wanted the part very badly. And, thank God, it worked out.

I met Charlie, who stands next to me on line in

the movie and plays Mike, at the beginning of August 1984. It was the first time all the cast had been brought together. We went to do a group photograph near the Brooklyn Bridge. And in a situation like that you notice people because you're checking everybody out.

But it was Sir Richard who did it. He had a dinner for all of us a week after we started rehearsals and I was sitting across from him. There was an empty seat beside me and Sir Richard asked Charlie to take it and that's how we started really talking to each other. We'd exchanged a few words at rehearsal but basically we'd all had so many other things to think about there. Just getting comfortable, getting to know the choreography. And that was the last thing on your mind, meeting someone.

Charlie's a very special person. He became very special to me too. By the end of the movie we'd decided to live together and see where it went. We seemed very happy, we got along well. We did everything together and we were best friends.

Klinger was playing Maggie the first time I saw *A Chorus Line* at the Schubert Theater. Although, at that juncture, I had by no means decided to accept the offer to direct the movie, I was sure of one thing. If I did, Klinger would play in it.

She had the most enchanting little figure, the looks of an angel, she moved beautifully and she sang like a lark. Let's face it. It was love at first sight.

In the event, however, it wasn't as easy as that. There were more possibilities for Maggie than for any other part in the movie. And many of them were of a very high standard indeed. But nobody else quite matched Klinger's combination of talents and, although we tested four or five other girls, in my estimation she remained consistently in the lead.

Maggie has a sad little story to tell but, equally, she has moments of fantasy and delight which, if not properly played, could be a little mawkish. Klinger has the face of a Madonna and such an absolute belief in the story that she's telling that it becomes very touching. With the addition of her crystal clear, perfectly pitched soprano singing voice, Maggie's moment in the picture is, I think, truly memorable.

Dressing 'the line' was a very complex matter. The characters didn't just appear and then exit. They stood in position for the entire length of the movie and therefore the combination of style and colors was terribly important.

Some performers are totally obsessed by what they are to wear. Of course, it's very understandable, particularly with girls, particularly in dancers. But Klinger was the easiest of them all. She was quite content – with the exception that she would have preferred the stripes on her pants to have been vertical rather than horizontal – to accept Faye's ideas and my final decision about the costume. I knew from the word go how I wanted her to look and that's how it turned out.

Audrey Landers

VAL

Film
Underground Aces (co-starred as Anne Wenders)

Leads in TV Series and Specials
Dallas (co-starring as Afton Cooper)
The Hitchhiker – Split Decision, HBO
Highcliffe Manor, NBC TV
Somerset, daytime drama (starring as Heather Kane) NBC
The Secret Storm, daytime drama (starring as Joanna Morrison) CBS

Variety
Audrey Landers, Her Music, European TV Special Christmas
Audrey Landers, Music is My Life, European TV
Soap Opera Special, MC
From Hawaii With Love, co-host with Glenn Campbell

Recordings
Ariola Records, 1983-5, 10 Gold Records, 1 Platinum Double LP
throughout Europe

*E*motionally, it was a hard time for me. I was very well known in New York but I couldn't get any work in California because I wasn't sexy enough. It was just confusing, frustrating and disappointing. I didn't know what I was doing wrong.

Since the age of twelve I'd been appearing in soaps and commercials on the East Coast and I was real wholesome with freckles from going out in the sun. But here I was in sunny California and the image they wanted was sexy.

So I started to wear big, shady hats and gave myself a certain time limit. I told my mother if I didn't get something that stayed on the air, something rewarding and enjoyable, I'd go back to New York at the end of August. This was 1980.

On July 17 I had an audition for a show called *Dallas*. It had been on the air about a year and a half but I'd never seen it. So I watched six hours of video tape before the audition.

And then came the decision about what to wear. In the end my sister loaned me her lucky dress. And, as I didn't know you could get padded bras, I wore three ordinary ones. I went to the audition and sat down to wait with probably four hundred girls. All different types and all for one episode of the same part.

The next day, at seven in the evening, they told me I'd been chosen. It was my twenty-second birthday. I was so excited. I didn't know how long I'd be on, or whatever. But there was a chance they'd pick up my character and make it bigger.

On what was virtually my first day, I was a little nervous. There was a piano on the set and in the lunch hour, when the whole studio was empty, I just started fooling around on it to calm myself, working on a song I was writing at the time.

The next thing I knew they called me into the producer's office and said would I mind playing and singing for them later that afternoon? They stopped filming for about ten minutes while I gave a little show. From that time on, they decided they would keep my character and make her an aspiring singer.

As a child I had two goals. I wanted to be a performer or I wanted to be a doctor. I have a BA in psychology from Columbia University in New York which means I could get a job in a clinic. But I couldn't practise as a psychiatrist. That would take another eight years of study.

My mother was a model and I got my first taste of show business when my sister and I would go with her on assignments. My Mom and I, we did a bubble bath commercial together when I was three. So I've had show business in my blood forever. Then my parents got divorced and Mom was on her own with two children to raise. And show business not being all that stable, she drifted away from it and started a printing company which is now very successful.

My Mom is really and truly responsible for helping me get this far. We kind of support each other's dreams. The reason that we're so close is that we've faced our struggles together. My sister and I have never rebelled because it's hard to rebel against somebody on the same level as you are. We are a team. We are best friends. And she also happens to be our mother. People who don't know her say, 'Oh, she must be one of those stage mothers, pushing and so forth.' But it's not like that at all.

I do want to get married and also start a family. I wouldn't stop working but I do want that duality. I think it's the balance that's missing in my life right now. What would happen if I fell in love with a guy my mother hated? I would listen to her with an open mind, knowing she's had more experience than I've had and she's only looking out for my best interests. If what she said didn't make any sense to me, then I think she would allow me to make a mistake. She'd just stand back and be ready to catch me when I fell.

It's rough on relationships when you travel as much as I do. Between July of '84 and July of '85, I spent only three and a half weeks at home. But the strangest thing was that while we were making *A Chorus Line* it was an opportunity to be with my boyfriend because he lives in New York. We'd had a bi-coastal romance for two years prior to that and we hadn't realised it could be so wonderful together. But then I had to leave when the movie was finished and he just couldn't deal with me not being there. We couldn't work it out.

I saw the show of *A Chorus Line* in my early teens and there was only one thing I remembered about it through all the years and that was sitting in the audience with my mother and when this girl sang the words, 'tits and ass', I almost fell off my chair. I told my mother I thought it was lewd and how could they say such things in a public theater?

Then, in the summer of 1984, my Mom and I flew into New York from France and got a message for me to go and meet Sir Richard, Cy and Ernie. On the way, we had the limousine stop to pick up a cassette of the show soundtrack and I listened to it on my Walkman. They'd told me that the number I had to sing for my test was called 'Dance Ten, Looks Three' and I went through the whole tape looking for it. And then I said, 'Oh, my God! It's *that* number!'

And I have to tell you, it wasn't easy to sing those words, even in the movie. I had to stand in front of the mirror, saying them as loud as I could, to make it seem natural for Val. Because, to her, it's not dirty language, it's just the way she talks. She does it so openly there's certainly nothing sexual about it. She's showing the world her new body from plastic surgery but she's showing it like a new hat or dress. She's saying, 'I'm still the same girl, I'm still that ugly little girl on the inside who was funny and gawky and wanted to be a great dancer. But you want T and A? Fine. I'll give you T and A.'

Personally, I wouldn't have plastic surgery. I don't like anything that's unnatural. I don't even like to take aspirin. I'm a kind of health food nut. I don't take any drugs. I don't smoke and the only drink I ever have, once in a while, is a little champagne.

But, for other people, if someone is really unhappy or insecure about their looks and plastic

surgery is going to change their personality and make them a happier person, I think that's fine.

★ ★ ★

One of the ways in which we endeavoured to keep the atmosphere from becoming too oppressive was to have visitors who could watch shooting from the balcony of the theater. As the weeks passed, to drop in on our set almost became *de rigueur* for anyone passing through New York and our guests included Michael Jackson, Roger Moore, Donald Sutherland, Richard Crenna, Marisa Berenson, Al Pacino and Burt Reynolds. To my delight, since I am a devoted admirer, Placido Domingo came in one day at Audrey's invitation *(see opposite).*

Amazingly enough, we found Val exceedingly difficult to cast. One knew exactly what one was looking for but, in a strange way, it seemed almost unattainable, although we'd tested several girls.

Val, as she tells Zach, is twenty-four and it seemed important to us that this should be credible, since she's obviously telling the truth. She not only had to look absolutely right, she also had to have the ability to perform. I don't just mean act. If she could act as well, that was a bonus. But, of all the numbers in the movie, 'Dance Ten, Looks Three', or 'Tits and Ass' as it's known, has to be sung by a sort of vaudeville performer, and we couldn't find her. We were getting very close to production and were in a degree of despair. Then, one morning, in marched somebody called Audrey Landers.

Now, I must have been living on some kind of desert island for the past six or seven years or maybe I'm outside the age range that's devoted to soap operas on the box so her name, I must confess, didn't ring a bell. And in came this little blonde bombshell – high heels, exquisite figure, hair falling round her shoulders, prettiest little face and laughing eyes.

I thought, 'Wow! That's an attractive girl.' But I was busy doing something else in another office. Cy and Ernie interviewed her and Cy finally came in to me and said, 'I don't think this is going to be any good but out of courtesy you should come and meet the young woman.'

I went in, rather displeased at being interrupted, and, for the first few minutes, still had my mind on other matters while the others talked to her. Slowly, however,

she captured my attention and I decided to test her.

Audrey came through like gangbusters. There was no question whatsoever, she could knock hell out of the number and here was another of those magical personalities who would simply burst upon you, once placed in front of a camera.

She was aware from the beginning that we had already cast fifteen of the best dancers in America and that she wasn't in that category at all. 'But I'll work,' she said. And, my God, did she work.

I think Audrey deserves her success as much as anybody I've ever come across. I came to love her very much and think that if she can find other areas to explore and finally conquer, as a performer, she has a huge career beyond even the one in which she is already eminently successful.

Terrence Mann

LARRY

Broadway
Cats (Rum Tum Tugger)
Barnum (Ringmaster)

National Company
Barnum (Ringmaster and P. T. Barnum), Nederlander Organization

Off-Off-Broadway
Night at the Fights (Ensemble)
Queen's Diamond (Rochefort)
Twelfth Night (Feste)

Regional Theater
A Midsummer Night's Dream (Oberon) & *Merchant of Venice* (Lorenzo)
Taming of the Shrew (Petrucchio) *Romeo and Juliet* (Tybalt)
The Rivals (Fag), *The Importance of Being Earnest* (Jack), *Servant of
Two Masters* (Arlecchino), *Summer and Smoke* (John)

Television
Search for Tomorrow, CBS, *One Life to Live*, ABC

Special Skills
Keyboards, percussionist, fight choreographer, juggler, unicyclist,
teeterboard, wire walker

All of a sudden, at fifteen or sixteen years old in high school, I was really neat. I was so cool. I became part of the 'in' group that year. I was invited to all these parties, to be in the Key Club and I got a girlfriend who was head of the Year Book staff.

All of a sudden ... because I was the star of *My Fair Lady*. They'd asked me to play Henry Higgins when the guy who was going to do it suddenly switched schools. I had to learn the whole thing in like two and a half weeks. I did it, the bug bit me and I said, 'This is fun.'

After two years in college, I applied to North Carolina School of the Arts for a four-year acting course. But after two years they kicked me out. I loved performing but I was really young and crazy, smoked pot, ran around, had a good time and got in a lot of trouble. I was a bad boy. When they kicked me out I broke into the office to look at my file. It said on my sheet, 'A lot of raw talent but undisciplined. We don't know whether he'll make it or not.'

I went to Florida for eighteen months with my girlfriend and that was the most terrible time. My grandmother, who I was very close to, died. My girlfriend had a drug problem and I had to put her in a rehabilitation center and they wanted me to go in too. I didn't because I was never heavily into drugs, ever in my life.

But I was beginning to think maybe I'm crazy and I'm having a nervous breakdown. I had finished performing altogether and had to get a job as a car jockey. The rock 'n roll band we'd formed went surely but slowly downhill until we ended up playing at dives on the beach. My luck had bottomed out.

Emotionally, mentally, spiritually, professionally, creatively, I was broke. The final coup on the whole decline was that I moved back in with my parents and caught a bad case of shingles.

Then I got a letter from a friend inviting me to join him on his farm. By March 1975 I'd saved enough money to get up there with my dog and stay two months in this log cabin. We built outhouses, grew our own food and just generally got in touch with the things that are really important. I put my life back together and literally, from then on, things just turned around.

I went for a weekend, back to the theater where I'd worked summers when I was in college. I was standing at the back, wishing, hoping, praying I could get a job in the theater again but knowing I couldn't because the season had already been cast. Then this hand comes up and taps on my shoulder and, before I can turn around, a voice says, 'Want a job?'

It was Mavis Rae, a dancer from Broadway who teaches in North Carolina. It was from her I got a lot of my dance training.

I said, 'I sure do.'

'I'll see you in two days,' she said and walked away. It was like she knew.

This was the Lost Colony company which performs outdoor dramas about historical events all over the country. I did it for the summer and, after working for the rest of the year as director of a children's theater, had another summer there. Then I went back to school.

At the School of the Arts … they accepted me again.

It was like the prodigal son had come home because I was scholarshipped all the way through and I graduated first in my class. I also won the Keenan Scholarship which is awarded to the actor they think is going to make it.

A Chorus Line is my first movie. After doing two big shows on Broadway, *Barnum* and *Cats*, I discovered that, in movies, the closer you are to yourself as a person, the more truthful you are, the better you're going to come across.

Richard has fun directing movies. You sense that on the set. He's there to have a good time and he's there to work seriously. He sets up the parameters for everybody and it's one of the healthiest situations, creatively, that I've been in. You get the right amount of fun, the right amount of humor and then it's time to be serious and get down to work. He's an inspiration and the main thing I've learned from *A Chorus Line* is to work better.

My character, Larry, the assistant choreographer, is the utility man, the one who gets the grease on his hands. He oils the machine that makes it work. You see him feeling for everybody, understanding what the people on 'the line' are going through, what Zach is going through, what Cassie is going through. He's trying to make two people who once loved each other very much not to be at odds with each other, not hate each other and especially, for God's sake, not in the middle of the most awful situation possible … an audition.

*I*n the movie, there was one part which, although it had to relate to the group as a whole – like Zach – also had to stand in its own right, needing considerable presence and weight. That was the part of Larry.

In the play he's a relatively insignificant character but since Arnold's script requires scenes to be played in the dressing room, in the prop room, by the stage door and so on, Larry becomes a catalyst. The majority of scenes off the stage find him as the pivotal figure. This means that, in addition to credibility as a sufficiently good dancer to demonstrate Zach's choreography, he also needs to be played by a smashing actor.

Julie and Barry presented a whole list of fascinating personalities but Cy had seen *Cats* and was bowled over by Terry Mann's performance as Rum Tum Tugger. And once I met him, I felt that unquestionably he was the leading contender.

He was an eminently capable dancer and patently, the moment he read, an absolutely first-rate actor. And he has the most mesmeric face. If you examine Terry's features they're not composed of what one assumes to be the ingredients for an attractive, interesting, intelligent face. Yet, taken as a whole, they evoke precisely that. You don't have to spend much time getting to know Terry's face. Bang! It arrives and, boy, once it arrives you can't watch anyone else.

It's another of those marvelous flukes of personality which translate supremely well to the screen. I was stupid enough to think it only worked with the camera but, having subsequently seen his performance in *Cats*, I realised he has the same impact onstage.

He has a star personality and if someone was prepared to give him a break, a really big break, Terry has the potential for a massive career in the theater and in film. Certainly he has endowed Larry with an individual characterisation that is absolutely captivating and I predict he will receive enormous attention once the picture opens.

Charles McGowan

MIKE

Films
Grease II (featured), Paramount
The Right Moves (Featured), Highgate Pictures
Annie, Columbia

Television
Out of Step, ABC, *Midnight Special*, NBC, *Portrait of a Stripper*,
ABC, *Golden Globe Awards*, CBS, *People's Choice Awards*, ABC, *Mike
Douglas*, CBS, *D. J. Awards*, ABC, *Grace Jones Special*, Mexico.

Regional Theater
George M! (George M. Cohan)
Oklahoma (Will Parker)
West Side Story (Action)
Gypsy (Tulsa)
Anything Goes (Purser)
Cabaret (asst. choreographer)
Damn Yankees (choreographer)
Dreamstreet (Chaz)

Special Skills
Piano, accordion, drums, martial arts and weapons, singing,
all sports, dancing.

I was born in San Francisco and the lady who gave birth to me put me up for adoption immediately because of this physical handicap I had. Well, I had a few. I had what's called a bladder extrophy which means I was not completely formed from the belly button down. Also, I did not have a pubic bone which is what keeps your feet straight and I was born with one abnormally small kidney.

This lady nurse who became my mother, Mrs McGowan, was working in pediatrics, and she saw something in my eyes. That's what she told me. The doctors had given up hope that I would ever walk because, at that time, there was nothing they could do.

The other lady, my natural mother, I don't think she cared. The way I was told, she didn't really want me. I went to court when I was three years old, and the judge asked me who I would like to live with. I remember sitting in the courtroom and briefly, vaguely, seeing her there. Her hair was kind of reddish brown.

Now I'm not so much interested in meeting her but I am interested in my physical background. Why I was born this way. If she used any kind of drugs or whether it's hereditary. If I have any brothers or sisters, biologically. I don't even know if she was married. I have no inkling of a father in the picture there.

So Mrs McGowan took me into her legal guardianship and gave me physical therapy, exercising my legs. I'd had my first operation when I was eighteen months old for reconstructive work on my bladder. They changed all the plumbing. I began walking when I was four. We lived in a Victorian house in San Francisco and my mother walked me up the stairs every day. I was a little kid, very small.

Then she put me into dancing to strengthen my legs and, as a result, what I have now is muscle instead of pubic bone. That helped, in a sense, with ballet but there was extreme pain, a lot of pain. When I had groin tears it took longer to heal than in someone else. That was a little rough. But dancing is an exercise I need to do.

I'm very familiar with hospitals because I was in and out every year. I dreaded summers because every one I'd have an operation. I've had eighteen, so far.

Mrs McGowan is one of a kind. They don't make mothers like that any more. She raised so many kids. It was a foster home ... plus. She took care of a lot of kids and she was a nurse at the same time. The kids all had something physically wrong with them. One was allergic to everything in the world. Another was a heroin baby. One of the children was burned severely. So all of the kids, about ten of us, worked together. We didn't dwell on our problems. We weren't like 'woe is me' and using that as a crutch.

Our mother could be very tough. Old-fashioned ways. Wow, did we have problems when I was in my teens. But, growing up, I learned to appreciate her toughness. Anybody weaker would have given up on me through those times and I wouldn't be where I am today. She's in her late seventies now. To earn extra money she used to sew for people, and she still does. That's what she lives on as well as her husband's pension

from the army. He became my Dad but he passed away in front of me when I was ten years old.

Dancing became more than a therapy when I did my first performance. I was quite young and I enjoyed the attention. It was like when I'd walked for the doctors the first time, a thrill to see their reaction. They'd applauded and given me popsicles. I started to really enjoy dancing because the more I did it, the happier I made people. I just learned to show off a lot. When I was eleven I began to take it seriously, but I wasn't aware that it could become my profession.

My Mom was, though. She had it planned. She knew exactly what I was going to do. She knew that dancing or performing was what I was here for. I wanted to play sports and things and that was when we got into disagreements, in my teens, and she said, 'No, no, no.'

I was at that age when I knew more than my mother and I just quit dancing for a while. Then it dawned on me when I was around seventeen, 'Hey, you're a very fortunate young man, don't throw it all away.' Some sports were hurting my body rather than being of any benefit.

I've known Jeffrey Hornaday for quite a while and I guess he hasn't met anybody else like me. It wasn't just dancing because I did sports . . . everything. So when this movie came about the character of Mike fitted. The song I sing is 'I Can Do That', Mike can do it. Put his mind to it, *he could do it* and in choreographing my dance Jeffrey basically let me do all the things I'm capable of doing if I put my mind to it. Some things I couldn't do right off the bat. But I told him I could learn them. Given some time. So he went ahead and we worked together on the number in that way.

I first heard about the movie when I was in Las Vegas doing a pre-Broadway show and I said to myself, 'Self, you've got to do this.'

I had auditioned for the play a few times and been blown away by the casting director for stupid reasons. I was furious. So when I heard about the movie I flew back to LA and went to all the big cattle calls. And it was not just because I knew Jeffrey that I got it. When I finally heard I didn't celebrate or anything, I just took a deep breath and said, 'Okay, don't blow it.'

It took three days to film the 'I Can Do That' number. It was like a marathon run. You hit the wall and the pride and the love and the having fun. Those three days will be with me forever. As well as the movie. I've thought about doing a number like that since I was in fourth grade. My dream came true for those three days.

Sir Richard left how long I could go on dancing up to me. He'd say, 'Er, Chuck, darling, we can go on to other things if you're feeling too exhausted.'

But something inside me just wanted to keep going. The adrenalin was flowing. I didn't want to let me down. I just wanted to do it. We all have our own dreams and fantasies. And I had a ball doing that.

I don't know how much longer I will dance because it's really taking a toll on me. Choreography is probably down the road. Not right now, but later.

What I would really like to do when I can't dance

any more is work with physically handicapped people, children or adults. I hate to use that word, handicapped, because it's an obstacle you have to overcome. The word. But, either through my dance or just talking or being there to listen, I would like to help.

★ ★ ★

There was one person Jeffrey was absolutely certain he wanted in the film, right from the beginning, and that was Chuck. They both come from the West Coast and Jeffrey believed that, with the number 'I Can Do That', there was an opportunity to demonstrate Chuck's unique ability as a dancer.

He's a personality dancer. He doesn't just dance as such. Chuck's a clown as well and he performs in a way that I've never seen before and which nobody could imitate. It's so spectacular and so very individual.

The movie's impact, after a big ensemble opening, depends on his song and dance number, as the first solo, and Chuck brings it off miraculously.

'I Can Do That' only occupies 3 minutes and 14 seconds of screen time. To take three days to shoot it may, therefore, appear an extravagance. But, by virtue of its pyrotechnic form, it had to be filmed in very brief takes, each of only a few seconds' duration, and all requiring the same meticulous rehearsal, lighting and preparation as a shot lasting several minutes. This is very tiring for the actor/dancer. Also Chuck's movements were so fast, almost frenetic, that, poor devil, he had to do it over and over again because the camera could barely be operated fast enough to follow him. Without Tom Priestley, I doubt we could have captured the number on film.

You only have to read Chuck's own story to have an inkling of what his life has been. And, having started with what were thought to be hopeless physical disabilities, his brilliant sustained athletic dancing is truly nothing short of phenomenal.

He's a remarkable chap altogether. One day he scared us all to death. The metal staircase backstage at the theater was rather gloomy and Chuck, having been woken from a doze, pelted down it for rehearsal and slipped … He fell and hurt himself quite badly. And when one knows of his physiology it is understandable that a fall involving the pelvic area could be very dangerous indeed. The paramedics were called and he was strapped to a stretcher and taken to hospital by ambulance. We were all devastated. But Chuck's commitment and determination to get back, get on form, was such that I should never had doubted he would do it. He is extremely disciplined, like most dancers, and he brings to the character of Mike a very special personality.

He became devoted to Klinger and she to him. Life isn't easy for anybody in our business. But with all the problems that Chuck has already overcome and the difficulties that Klinger will encounter due to the fact that she is primarily considered a singer, if their relationship works out, they'll cope with the life far more successfully as a couple than either would alone.

Alyson Reed

CASSIE

Broadway
Marilyn (Marilyn)
Dancin' (Featured)
Oh Brother (Fatatatatatima)
Dance a Little Closer (Elaine)

National Tour
A Chorus Line (Cassie & Val)
Pippin (Catherine)

Television
Ziegfeld: The Man and His Women, NBC
Johnny Mann Series (Pilot), KTLA
200 Years Ago Today, Public Service

Film
'10' (solo ballet/double Bo Derek), MGM

Regional Theater
Damn Yankees (Gloria), *Side by Side by Sondheim*, *Applause* (Eve),
Festival (All Femme Roles), *Bells Are Ringing*, *Barbary Coast* (featured),
Sweet Charity (Charity), *Music Man* (Marian), *Oliver* (Nancy)

I was petrified when I had to play a scene in bed with Michael Douglas. Because I'd never done anything like that before. But it turned out that the little demon in my head was far worse than anything that happened. It became so technical. Like being told when you're kissing that you're out of your key light and you should move two inches to your left.

After a while I said to the crew, 'Boy, if I knew it was this difficult, I'd give it up at home.'

Cassie, the part I play, is a lot of what Alyson would like to be. In the film, unlike the show, she's not self-pitying. She makes her choices. She's a real work horse of the dance world, a person that has worked her way up, paid her dues and done her homework. Someone who demonstrates that part of the human spirit which can choose, in an intense situation, either to laugh at how ludicrous it is or play into its intensity and make herself miserable. Cassie manages to laugh at the embarrassing situation she's created which, I think, is very daring, very brave.

I know that if it were not for Richard, I would never have done this role. He really pushed for me. I'm not only indebted on that level but because he made me believe in myself the way he believed in me. I've been told that, during the casting, it came to a point where he said, 'Either Alyson Reed does this, or I don't.'

One of the nice things when we had an early meeting is that he said, 'We're both the same. We kind of know each other, don't we?'

And I said, 'Yes, we do.'

Before we started shooting we had quite a few dinners together and I just picked his brain. I believe that without knowledge there's a lot of fear. Since all my training had been for the stage, I kept asking him about all the technical things to do with film.

He said, 'Well, first you have to trust me implicitly. I'm your audience.'

In the beginning that was so frustrating for me. I'm real good at reading an audience but all of a sudden there was nothing to read.

And the other thing he told me was, 'If you're telling the truth, none of the technicalities matter. And if you're not, you're in big trouble. You always have to tell the truth on film.'

He explained that any time you speak it's always preceded by a hundred thoughts that happen in the blink of an eye. Most of the time you're not even aware of them. And what really counts in film is whether the thought process, getting to that emotion, is also available to the audience. Even when you're only listening to someone else you have to *really* listen, answering in your mind. I found that the more I could have an internal dialog going on, the more exciting it was on film. That was the thing I really loved by the end, once I had the confidence.

I remember playing the scene where Cassie first comes onto the stage in her leotard and it's obvious that Zach is shocked because he's seeing her body after so long, the whole thing. I came walking out thinking, 'Oh, my God. My legs are too fat. I'm not in shape. What's going on in his mind? I'm sure he thinks I look like hell.' Going through all the thoughts an insecure person would have instead of just 'playing' insecure.

I started the film with one day of exteriors in September. Because I didn't have any lines it reminded me of doing a commercial and I told myself, 'This is going to be a piece of cake.'

Richard said, 'Doesn't anything unnerve you?'

But then I had three and a half weeks off and in that time I had an anxiety attack that lasted forty-eight hours. I couldn't sleep and I couldn't eat anything. I just freaked out. Because of fear.

I was doing the lead that practically every female in the business wanted. It was going to be seen by the whole world, not just New York audiences. I was working with *Sir* Richard Attenborough and doing the longest running musical in history. I was working in a medium that I knew nothing about. The whole thing, the responsibility, just kind of hit me. My fear came to the surface and I just froze.

So I started going on the set when they were shooting the opening sequence. And that relaxed me a lot because I saw how things worked. I can't imagine how awful it must be not to trust the director, to be in a film where you have a bad director or someone who sees things totally differently and having to do battle all the time.

All of our emotions were so readily available to Richard because of nerves and fear and insecurity, and that was to his advantage. He is so good at playing people and so good at knowing what makes each individual tick that he could use it, either by calming someone's fears or by letting them come up at different times. It was great having a director who had been through the same process as an actor and knew about the insecurities. He got to understand me so well that he knew how to play me. And I'd let him. I'd let him do it.

The film changed a lot of things for me, not only professionally but in my personal life too. I found, when it was over and I started back into my daily living, that I had grown without knowing it. I hadn't seen the process because I was so engulfed, so involved. All of a sudden I was a different Alyson and I was reaching down to call on the same strengths and weaknesses and everything had been re-arranged. I grew up and I don't really know when it happened. I'm not saying it all happened during the film but I think that was the catharsis.

I was depressed for two weeks after we finished shooting. You spent seven months of concentrated effort with the same people. They saw you sick, with no make-up. They saw you in good moods. They saw every side of you: the times you were crying, when you started your period, when you had the flu. They became family. To cut the umbilical cord all of a sudden was very hard.

I will never, never forget the final night of the shoot. It should have been all twenty of us having a cry and hugging each other and the crew. But 'the line' had finished a week earlier. The very last shot was a close-up of Michael, watching me dance. And then suddenly it was over and Richard said, 'Print it. That's a

wrap, gentlemen. Thank you. Thank you very much.'

And I remember standing there in disbelief, saying, 'That's it?'

★ ★ ★

Choosing Cassie was the subject of much debate. Alyson is right in what she has said – and it's typical of her honesty – that the decision to cast her was by no means unanimous.

Everybody else undoubtedly had their own particular image of how the part should be played. Just as you have your own concept of Eliza in *My Fair Lady*, or Dolly in *Hello, Dolly*, so people have very fixed ideas as to what Cassie in *A Chorus Line* should be.

I, being at an advantage or a disadvantage, had none. I came to Cassie in the same way that I came to Zach: purely from the point of view of the movie. This is because the principal departure from the show is a series of flashbacks to Cassie and Zach's life before the present-day story begins. And so her personality has to be created, or at the very least reshaped for the film.

Because *A Chorus Line* is almost Broadway folklore, an American director might have had a certain trepidation in departing from the original. But, rightly or wrongly, I did not feel Cassie was sacrosanct.

I felt that she should be in her late twenties. She should, without question, be intelligent and have a very marked personality of her own, kooky elfin, tomboyish. One could not define the parameters in isolation. To a degree, particularly when casting a fictitious character, one should allow the personality of the player to impinge and embroider upon the role.

And of all the actresses that we saw, interviewed and, indeed, tested Alyson seemed to me an absolute standout. I felt she could bring to Cassie a strength, a fascination and a series of individual traits which were, in my experience so far, unique.

She tested at first for Val and, oddly enough, that counted as much in my decision to cast her as Cassie as did her test for the actual part. It displayed a sense of humor, almost of self-mockery, which I felt was vital because, without it, Cassie could become self-pitying.

Alyson is not a conventional beauty in the normal movie sense. But, in common with other people who have seen her in the film, I think she is a totally, fascinatingly attractive woman.

Alyson's exceptional talents are most evident in 'Let Me Dance For You' which is the new number Marvin and Ed wrote for the end of the movie. We decided, by virtue of its lyric content, that it should be part song, part dance and part dramatic scene. And Alyson in that number brought the set to a standstill with spontaneous applause from the crew.

A movie director, if he's worth his salt, must retain the right of decision and must ultimately, right or wrong, stand by his conviction. I felt absolutely certain in my own mind that Alyson was the one person who could successfully pull off the part of Cassie. Having taken the gamble and on seeing the whole film put together, I am more than ever convinced.

Justin Ross

GREG

Broadway
A Chorus Line (Gregory Gardner)
Pippin (Lewis)
The Magic Show (Steve)
Encore – Radio City Music Hall (Principal)
Got To Go Disco (King)

Off-Broadway
Fortune (Roscoe)

Regional Theater
More Than You Deserve
Feathertop
On the Road to Babylon
Flop
Rocky Horror Show (Dr Frank N'Furter)

Film
The Fan

I got a phone call that morning from a girlfriend whose cat was pregnant. 'Justin, get over here immediately. The cat is pushing out the first kitten. Please come over. I have to leave for rehearsal.'

So I go there and, of course, the whole household is in total uproar. The cat is giving birth and in pain and there's this little kitten on the floor and it's a mess and my girlfriend has her coat on. She's trying to get out of the house and I'm sitting there going, 'Oh, my God, what do I do? What do I do?'

And she's handing me a book. 'This is how you cut the umbilical cord and this is what you do with the hot water if need be ...'

All these instructions and I'm a nervous wreck. And the phone rings and it's my agent.

'You've got the movie.'

Well, by this time the cat had given birth to a second kitten. You know those moments when everything in your head is booming like a gong and it's like you're not sure you heard because the blood is pounding? I went, 'Oh, God. Oh, my God, that's great but ... but ... the cat is dragging the baby around by the umbilical cord.' He's going, 'What the hell are you talking about? You got the movie.'

I said I'd talk to him later. I hung up the phone and I'm standing there going: 'Be calm, be calm, be calm.' And the cat stopped dragging the kitten around and started doing what nature intended. Now I'm in a strange house. There's a cat with two kittens, ready to give birth to a third. And total silence ...

And I thought, did I get a phone call that said I had the movie? It was like being in the twilight zone. I swore I wasn't going crazy. But ...

Then the phone rang again. 'Hello, Justin, this is Dickie Attenborough. I would like very much for you to be in the movie.'

I hung up the phone and again I was sitting there all by myself. I mean this was like one of the most momentous phone calls I'd ever got in my life and I was there all alone. I just wanted to scream.

I landed my first off-Broadway show in 1973. It was black comedy, a musical, about the Vietnam War. But people were not ready to laugh about that in the early Seventies and the reviewers either said it was extraordinary or the most disgusting, despicable thing they'd ever seen. I was completely wrapped in bandages from head to toe and tap-danced to a song called, 'How Would You Like to Marry a Man Without a Face?'

In my next show I played a neuron in a musical that took place in someone's brain... But, as a friend of mine said, they should have been more concerned about the musical that took place on the stage.

Then I was in *The Magic Show* and again I was covered from head to toe in a very bizarre costume. Three productions in a row and nothing showed but my eyes, my nose and my mouth. I wondered if they were trying to tell me something.

The show of *A Chorus Line* opened in 1975 and I went into it in 1976. It was, to say the least, the most thrilling time of my life. I stayed with it then, the first

time, for just over two years. It was a wonderful show to be in because of the prestige and the respect and all that. Because it was so wonderful I didn't get bored with it for a good year. Then I started to go.

On many levels it's a difficult show to do. Greg, as a character, is not very well developed. You stand on line interminably, always listening and reacting. Then you step forward and you talk to Zach and when you step back you listen and you react some more. Night after night after night.

I thought, 'Hey, come on. You're appearing in this incredible Broadway show. Stop beefing. You're being paid a very good salary plus the fact that there's not very much else out there.'

So that kind of got me through another six months, and the last six months it was getting very difficult and then I said, 'It's just time for me to leave.' But I wasn't so much of a hero that I quit cold turkey. I had an industrial lined up.

A couple of years ago, I started thinking about what else I would like to do. I was going through a period of being disenchanted with the theater and I even thought about driving a cab or working as a salesperson.

I have to slap myself every now and again and just remember how fortunate I am. I do take it for granted sometimes. I do get caught up in bullshit. Any job, there are rules and regulations. But the fact that I can do what I dream about, have dreamed about all my life, and get paid well for it, is a gift, a quite extraordinary gift.

Greg is the one overtly gay character in the story and this gave rise to a great deal of thought because concepts of a homosexual character were completely different when the show opened from those that apply now. The very word 'gay' was not in everyday use at the time.

Second only to Val, Greg, I think, was the hardest part to cast. Justin I had seen in the show and he was terrific. He landed every single laugh that was there brilliantly. But when we tested him, there was a theatricality about his performance which was totally unacceptable.

However, there were so many attributes in his personality that were right we finally decided to cast him. And thank heaven we did. Slowly, by detailed analysis of the difference between theater and film acting, Justin, without losing anything, pulled his performance down to a level that was correct for cinema.

By 'pulled down' I do not mean that the difference is only one of scale. There are other elements which determine a satisfactory performance on film, not the least of which is pure actor's concentration. That may appear relatively easy to achieve. It isn't.

If a performance is to stand in its own right rather than be re-shaped purely by cutting, concentration in terms of integrity and veracity is vital. What is terrific about Justin is that he endows Greg with the right degree of flair and flamboyance, but with a base of absolute reality, and, as a result, the character is not only funny, which he has to be, but he is also rather touching.

Blane Savage

DON

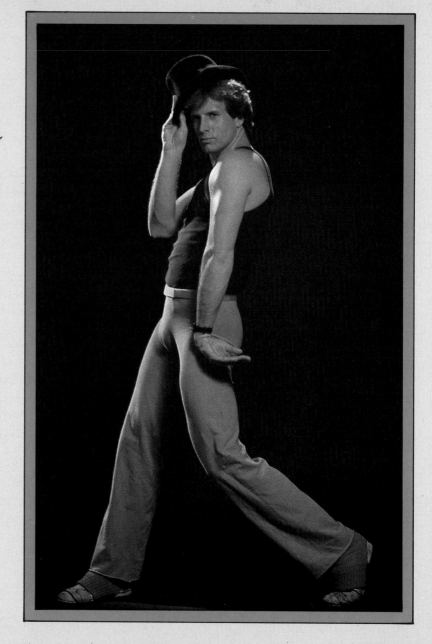

Broadway
Dancin' (originated role)

Television Films
Mae West (Frank Wallace)
Reach Out (Policeman)

Films
To Be or Not To Be, 20th-Century Fox
New York New York, MGM
Last Married Couple in America, Universal
Can't Stop the Music, MGM

Television
Musical Comedy Tonight (featured performer)
Fantasy Island (featured performer)
Bosom Buddies (featured performer)
Lynda Carter Special (featured peformer)

Regional Theater
Get Happy (originated role)
Perfectly Frank (taped for showtime)
Seven Brides for Seven Brothers (Frank)

The outside of Don is that he's married and he's got two kids and a mother he's supporting too. The inside of Don is he really doesn't want any of that. What Don would like to be, deep in his heart, is Blane. I've got money. I'm not married. I've got freedom. I can go anywhere in the world I want.

I started out in the chorus. Chorus. Chorus. Chorus. Ten thousand chorus jobs. Sixteen people, eight people, ten people. I remember being exhausted. Doing eight shows a week and constant, non-stop dancing. I remember changing clothes a thousand times, sweating, going onstage, coming offstage, changing clothes again and running back.

There is a kind of threshold of pain and tiredness that you have to break through. In sport they call it 'the wall'. You get to it and you have to go past it. I'm pretty much in pain all the time. I don't know anyone that's danced long enough—I've danced now for twenty years—who isn't. You're in constant pain. Even when you're on vacation, you're in pain. My knees hurt now. My ankles hurt. Normal people who do other jobs don't really have any idea of what a dancer goes through. So it's something that you really have to love.

Dancing holds a very special place in my heart. It brought me into manhood and it brought me out of a situation I didn't want to be in. I was very introverted and it gave me a form of self expression I might never have been able to find otherwise. In the beginning, I approached it from a sports attitude. I never thought of it as an art form. It was always a very physical, demanding sport. Since then I've refined it and, of course, it is an art form.

In the past two or three years I have pretty much been out of the chorus doing solo and featured work with parts here and there. Making the movie, I found myself in the chorus again and I found myself reflecting on the audition process. Jobs always came very easily to me, so I've never been through the kind of torture *A Chorus Line* is about. Before, I never really spent a great deal of time worrying about the people that didn't get the jobs. I always got the job. But, making the movie, I remembered the faces of people I've auditioned with for the last fifteen years and knew how they must have felt when they were rejected.

Everybody in this world wants a job. Our egos are wrapped up in work and getting paid for it. On a dancer's level, it means personal acceptance. When they don't get the job at auditions, it's a personal affront. It's not like somebody who sells toothbrushes. If they don't make a sale it's the toothbrush that's rejected. But actors and dancers, it's personal. It's, 'My God, they don't like *me*.'

And, in fact, it may not have anything to do with that. They may want somebody taller or shorter. They want somebody with a moustache. They want their girlfriend in the show. The problem with entertainers is that they go through it five times a week. It is a cruel business. It's a brutal, cruel business.

Dancers never want to talk about themselves. They want to dance. They express themselves through their bodies, their feet, their hands. They don't want to say anything. That's why so few of them go on to become actors. For me, the leaps were always very important. I love that type of expression, that feeling of freedom. To be able to jump and feel like you're never going to come down ...

I'm going to get emotional now. Ever since I started in this business I've always wanted to work with a Richard Attenborough. Not him necessarily but somebody who says, 'We'll take the time.'

When I worked on my monologue, it was so wonderful. He actually took the time to believe, to support, to give me that chance. He was in charge and cared enough to want to make it the best it could be. It was very refreshing to work with him. I'm sure he must have been a bundle of nerves himself. He was working on a major motion picture and the pressure must have been amazing, but he seemed able to put it aside.

I've always wanted to work with someone like him and I never have in fifteen years. I would dearly hope that if I ever get into a situation where I'm in charge, I could bring to it the qualities I learned from him. We've all worked on jobs where people are uncaring and crazy, 'Stand here. Go there. Do that.'

I can at last say that I've experienced working with someone who really cares. And it doesn't always have to be crazy. I was losing faith with the industry and with the way people were. He has reaffirmed my faith in what I'm doing. Even if that's all that comes out of the movie for me, it will be well worthwhile.

*T*he dilemma which always faces a director when presented with a character who has to be 'ordinary' is that the very make-up of an actor or actress, if they're any good, demands or results in the extraordinary. Although Arnold Schulman found a number of marvelous characteristics to make him more three-dimensional than in the stage play, this was essentially the dilemma we faced with Don.

We saw dozens and dozens of candidates but it wasn't until Blane came in to read for us that suddenly a light was thrown on this particular character. Blane is very good looking, physically very attractive. He is intelligent, highly disciplined and a marvelous dancer. He worked extremely hard, was always fully prepared and makes his own impact in the movie with a characterisation that is fully realised in its own right.

Blane is very generous about the atmosphere I attempt to create for actors. This stems from formative experiences with John Boulting when I too was in my twenties. John first directed me in *Journey Together* and, subsequently, helped me transfer a performance from theater to film with *Brighton Rock.* My understanding of that process emanates overwhelmingly from him.

One of the things that became evident during *A Chorus Line* is that Blane can be highly amusing. He's a first-rate *raconteur* and has an extraordinary ear. Should he choose to concentrate more on straight acting, I believe he could have a satisfying and successful career ahead of him.

Matt West

BOBBY

Broadway
A Chorus Line (Bobby)

Touring Company
Fiddler on the Roof (Sasha)
Peter Pan (Peter Pan), Walt Disney Production
Carmen Dragon tour (guest soloist)

Stock
Hello Dolly (Barnaby)
Bye Bye Birdie (Hugo)
Cactus Flower (Senor Sanchez)

Choreography
Numerous shows for Walt Disney Productions
Lido de Paris, Las Vegas, Line Captain

Television
Bernadette Peters Special (dancer), CBS
Tim Conway Special (dancer), CBS
Red Skelton Special (dancer), CBS
Home Town Christmas, Walt Disney Productions

She was Alice and I was the White Rabbit and she chased me round these giant teapots. We were both thirteen. The next year she was an ostrich and I was a dancing hippo wearing toe shoes.

That's how I first met Alyson, who plays Cassie in the movie. We both danced in the Christmas Parades at Disneyland, which was near our homes in California.

I started tap dancing when I was eight after I saw it on TV one night and wanted to take classes. My parents thought it was just a passing fancy and I'd get over it. But I never did. I was going five days a week when I first started, right after school. It drove my parents crazy.

Then the choreographer at the Christmas Parade told my mother that Disney Studios were looking for someone to portray Peter Pan on the road. They send out children's tours and you travel throughout the US on their private jet, *The Mickey*, doing all kinds of things to promote their films. And I did that for five years. As Peter Pan who never grows up. I tried very hard not to do that either ... but it didn't work.

So they decided to try me out as Christopher Robin with *Winnie the Pooh* but that didn't work either. I was too tall for him. Finally, what they did was put me back in Disneyland and I joined a singing group called Kids of the Kingdom. And there was Alyson! We were reunited again.

About that time, I guess it was 1977, Radio City Music Hall was going to be torn down and Disney decided to put up a lot of money to keep it going. So they produced the show that summer and sent me to New York. And while I was there I auditioned for *Fiddler on the Roof* and got the part of Sasha. And that's when I left Disney, after about seven years.

I was working as a dance captain in Las Vegas when I auditioned for the show of *A Chorus Line*. Three days later I was in Milwaukee rehearsing for the national tour. That was 1979. I played Don at first and then Mark. One night, I was somewhere in the US, Michael Bennett called and asked if I would come the next day and open on Broadway – as Bobby. So I packed up, flew out and played him onstage for the next four years. I only came out of the show when I was cast as Bobby in the movie. And guess who was the first person I saw at the dance auditions? Yes, it was Alyson.

Michael Bennett's choreography is very hard on the knees. Jeffrey Hornaday's is hard on the neck. Michael's is kind of sleazy and low to the floor – a lot from the waist down. In Jeffrey's you work from the waist up.

I'd done the show on Broadway for so long and, having taken only one week off before we started dance rehearsals for the movie, I was listening to the same music and trying to make my body go a completely different way. In the beginning it was very frustrating. But after a few weeks my body did start to relearn. It's a question of confidence. Suddenly you can do those head rolls and body waves and they look all right.

This is my first film and I feel that Sir Richard is a wonderful director because he was such a wonderful

actor. I'd heard so much about him before we started work. How understanding he was, how patient and sincere and all those things you believe can't possibly be true. But they are. Most other directors, Broadway directors, let's say, try to stay superior. Let you know that you're working for them and, if you don't do what they want, you'll be replaced. That wasn't the feeling on Sir Richard's set at all.

Over all the years, I have made Bobby into part of me. But we always did have a lot in common. I used to rearrange my parent's furniture when they'd go out to dinner. Just like Bobby. It's the truth. I used to get in so much trouble because I would bring in the lamps from the bedroom because I thought they'd look better with the front room furniture. And I'd also give garage recitals. My sister had to be all the female leads and my brothers would come in and be the male leads. I'd take my allowance for the week and buy kazoos so the kids in the neighborhood could be the orchestra. I wouldn't let anybody go home for dinner until we'd done rehearsing. They'd be screaming and my mother would open the garage door and take me out by the ear. I was in trouble a lot. But she did come in, sit down and endure every production that I put on.

When I was waiting to hear about the movie, my Mom said, 'As soon as it's positive, can I go up on the roof and scream?'

But when I called her, she cried on the phone. I cried on the phone. My Dad cried on the phone. And when I told Alyson, she cried too.

*M*att had the impertinence to nickname me 'Dad'. Together with Klinger and Justin, he was in the show's cast when I saw it in 1984. His characterisation of Bobby seemed absolutely right and the skilful way in which he delivered his major monologue was, I was sure, capable of being translated into cinema.

To me, he epitomises this extraordinary breed of performer, unique, indigenous to America, if not Broadway. He is the archetypal gypsy.

As long as I live, I shall never forget seeing the first night of *Oklahoma* at the Theatre Royal Drury Lane. That was nearly forty years ago, in the Forties. It was an absolute revelation to us in England that, together with jazz and the movies, another contemporary art form – the musical – resided in the United States. It is performers such as Matt who made that possible. He has considerable expertise in the triple combination of skills which every gypsy must possess.

I remember going backstage at the Schubert Theater to tell him that we were going to test him for Bobby. At one important moment in the movie he reflects the spontaneous joy he showed then. He is an actor who bases everything on truth and a thoroughly professional performer, which is not necessarily the same as merely having the talent to be one.

Over the seven months of rehearsals and shooting, I became devoted to the entire cast. The kids, I think, are a unique and totally exceptional group. We became like family. And none more so than Matt. I'm very proud of this particular son.

Post-Production

It's a combination of exhilaration and terror.

In early post-production, you're very much alone with the editor in the austere, workman-like surroundings of the cutting room. Around the walls, like the inside of a bees' nest, are brown, ten-inch-square boxes of film – the honey you've collected and stored over the previous months. The contrast between this atmosphere and that created by over a hundred crew and cast, all bursting with energy, while the film was being shot, is very marked.

If you have an editor of brillance, like Johnny Bloom, he will already have taken many of the initial steps in putting sequences together. There are always certain scenes which the editor can shape, almost regardless of the manner in which they've been shot. On the other hand, and particularly with a musical, there are constraints which impose a cutting pattern and, since I tend to shoot in a preconceived form, many sequences are destined to make their final appearance almost exactly as they were shot.

Nevertheless, there are always the surprises, the moments when the editor, by a stroke of masterly invention, transforms a scene into something beyond the director's wildest dreams. John, in shaping one part of the movie, suddenly lit up the cutting room with a staggering idea which had never even occurred to me. Some sequences do surprise and delight at this stage. Others, which you believed to be successful, prove disappointing on assembly. In either event, however, with a musical, a great deal of the finished result depends on the score, for which the concept and arrangement demand a very special talent.

Ralph Burns, I think, has a touch of genius. He's a diminutive man who constantly reminds me of Pinnochio's father in the Disney film, apparently tentative about putting forward his own ideas in preference to those of others and yet capable of insinuating judgments – which frequently prove irresistible – into any assessment of the contribution the music can make. A vast proportion of any success we may achieve will be due to him.

When we were fortunate enough to secure Ralph's services he made only one stipulation; that we should engage as music editor – the person responsible for physically matching the score to the picture – a young man called Michael Tronick. It was a proviso we learned to welcome. None of us working on the film have ever encountered a music editor of quite such talent.

We recorded the music in New York, together with additional singing and post-synchronised dialog lines – that is the re-recording, to match lip movements on the screen, of any words which are unclear or marred by extraneous noise or which could be improved in terms of interpretation. Most of the cast came back to add little pieces of sound, either sung or spoken, and it was wonderful to catch up on all their news. This process took us four weeks and, musically, our days ranged from those when we'd record only a single piano to others when the studio housed a full eighty-piece orchestra.

I have always dubbed my films at Twickenham Studios, just outside London, under the supervision of Gerry Humphreys: *A Chorus Line* was no exception. However, following previews on the West Coast, for various reasons we had no alternative but to continue the work in Hollywood. The credit for the final sound-track must therefore go not only to Gerry and his colleague, Robin O'Donoghue, but also the stalwart trio who took charge at Goldwyn Studios: Don Mitchell, Mike Minkler and Kevin O'Connell. Their joint effort is, I think, superb.

I don't, like some directors, need to feel the celluloid racing through my own fingers during post-production. My pinnacle of joy and, one has to say, on some occasions nadir of despair, comes towards the end – in the dubbing theater. We sit there in the dark, maybe eight or ten of us, under the watchful ear of Jonty Bates, the best of sound editors, immersed in the technical complexities of some forty or fifty kinds of sound being mixed to produce, ultimately, the single track that will accompany the movie. There follows, with the director of photography, the process of grading to determine the range of color tones that will appear on the screen. And when these two elements, the final sound track and the final version of picture, are put together, we have what's called a married print.

But the real marriage, if the movie is to work, is between it and the audience. And we shall begin to have an inkling as to whether this union is successful on 9 December 1985 when *A Chorus Line* has its world première, appropriately, at Radio City Music Hall in New York, before an audience that will include, as guests, the chorus of every show then running on Broadway.

Richard Attenborough
30 September 1985

Embassy Film Associates

and

Polygram Pictures

present a

Feuer and Martin Production

Richard Attenborough's

film

A Chorus Line

Based upon the stage play A CHORUS LINE conceived,
choreographed and directed by Michael Bennett

The book of the stage play was written by James Kirkwood and
Nicholas Dante

It was produced on the stage by Joseph Papp and was a New York
Shakespeare Festival Presentation

The Cast

Michael Blevins *as* Mark Michelle Johnston *as* Bebe
Yamil Borges *as* Morales Janet Jones *as* Judy
Jan Gan Boyd *as* Connie Pam Klinger *as* Maggie
Sharon Brown *as* Kim Audrey Landers *as* Val
Gregg Burge *as* Richie Terence Mann *as* Larry
Michael Douglas *as* Zach Charles McGowan *as* Chuck
Cameron English *as* Paul Alyson Reed *as* Cassie
Tony Fields *as* Al Justin Ross *as* Greg
Nicole Fosse *as* Kristine Blane Savage *as* Don
Vicki Frederick *as* Sheila Matt West *as* Bobby

with

Pat McNamara *as* Robbie Jennifer Kent *as* Reject dancer
Sammy Smith *as* Doorman Mansoor Najee-Ullah *as* Cab Driver
Timothy Scott *as* Boy with headband Reuben Sottomayor *as* Delivery boy
Bambi Jordan *as* Girl in yellow trunks Peter Fitzgerald *as* Dancer with gum
Richard DeFabees *as* Reject dancer June Eve Story *as* Dance teacher
Melissa Randel *as* Reject dancer John Hammil *as* Advertising executive
Jeffrey Cornell *as* Reject dancer Jack Lehnert *as* Posterman
Karen Prunczik *as* Reject dancer Gloria Lynch *as* Taxi passenger
  Gregg Huffman *as* Misfit boy dancer

The Dancers

Eric Aaron
Annemarie
Michele Assaf
Buddy Balou
Tina Bellis
Ida Broughton
Brian Bullard
Bill Bushnell
Sergio Cal
Linda Cholodenko
Christine Colby
Anne Connors
Jeffrey Cornell
Frank Cruz
Kim Darwin
John Deluca
Rickee Farrell
Penny Fekany
Angel Ferreira
Ed Forsyth
David Gibson
Darrell Greene
Tonda Hannum
Laura Hartman
Sonya Hensley
Linda Hess
Craig Innes
Reed Jones
Barbara Kovac
Andrew Kraus
Michael Lafferty
Barbara Lavorato

Mia Malm
Celia Marta
Liz McLellan
Gwendolyn Miller
Gregory Mitchell
Edd Morgan
Charles Murray
Arleen Ng
Alan Onickel
Peggy Parten
Helene Phillips
Richard Pierlon
Rhett Pyle
Vicki Regan
Tia Riebling
Debbie Roche
Adrian Rosario
Patricia Ruck
Mark Ruhala
Lynne Savage
Jeanna Schweppe
Jodi Sperduto
Leslie Stevens
William Sutton
Kirby Tepper
Evelyn Tosi
Linda Von Germer
James Walski
Marsha Watkins
Melanie Winter
Lily Lee Wong
Barbara Yeager

Khandi Alexander
David Askler
Bryant Baldwin
Carol Baxter
Robin Brown
Anna Bruno
Cheryl Burr
Roxann Cabalero
Joe Anthony Cavise
Cheryl Clark
Alexander Cole
Leslie Cook
Alice Cox
Amy Danis
Gary-Michael Davies
Anita Ehrler
Denise Faye
Felix
Scott Fless
William Gabriner
Sandra Gray
Michael Scott Gregory
Niki Harris
D. Michael Heath
Dawn Herbert
Regina Hood
Cindy Lauren Jackson
Bob Kellet
Stanley Kramer
Wayde Laboissoniere
Brett Larson
Rodney Alan MaGuire

Monique Mannen
Frank Mastrocola
Nancy Melius
Brad Miskell
Debi A. Monahan
Bob Morrisy
Ron Navarre
Reggie O'Gwyn
Lorena Palacios
Keri Lee Pearsall
Lacy Phillips
Scott Plank
Bubba Dean Rambo
Daryl Richardson
Michael Rivera
Leora Ron
Elissa Rosati
Michelle Rudy
George Russell
Ann Louise Schaut
Kimry Smith
Ty Stephens
Mary Ellen Stuart
Scott Taylor
Christopher Todd
David Vernon
Bobby Walker
Robert Warners
Faruma Williams
Scott Wise
Leslie Woodies

The Crew

PRODUCTION OFFICE
Associate Producer: Joseph M. Caracciolo
Production Office Co-ordinator: Jane Raab
Assistant: Jennifer W. Shore
Production Auditor: Kathleen McGill
Assistant Auditor: Matilde Valera
Payroll Auditor: Heidi August
Assistant to Richard Attenborough: Clare Howard
Assistants to the Producers: Lucy Cormack, Harriet Altmark
Location Manager: Clayton Townsend

ON THE SET
1st Assistant Director: Robert Girolami
Script Supervisor: B.J. Bjorkman
Assistant to the Director: Michael White
2nd Assistant Director: Louis d'Esposito
Additional 2nd Assistant Directors: Amy Sayres, James Skotchdopole
DGA Trainee: Jill Frank
Rehearsal Stage Manager: Phil Friedman
Production Assistant: Jane Paul
Assistant Choreographers: Brad Jeffries, Gregg Burge
Construction Grip: Joseph Williams Sr.
Property Master: Joseph Caracciolo Jr.
Head Carpenter: Carlos Quiles

CAMERA
Director of Photography: Ronnie Taylor B.S.C.
Camera Operator: Thomas Priestley Jr.
1st Assistant Cameraman: Hank Muller Jr.
2nd Assistant Cameraman: Gary Muller
Additional Camera: Richard Kratina, Peter Norman
Camera Trainee: Doug Pelligrino
Louma Crane Technician: Stuart Allen
Gaffer: Dick Quinlan
Best Boy: Robert Conners
Key Grip: Edwin Quinn
Dolly Grip: John Volpe

ART DEPARTMENT
Production Designer: Patrizia von Brandenstein
Art Director: John Dapper
Set Decorator: George DeTitta
Set Dresser: Marty Rosenberg

SOUND
Sound Mixer: Chris Newman
Boom Operator: Vito Ilardi
Recordist: Arthur Bloom
Playback Operator: Neil Fallon

WARDROBE
Costume Designer: Faye Poliakin
Wardrobe Supervisors: Jennifer Nichols, Bill Christians
Assistants to Faye Poliakin: Catou Guillard, Toyce Anderson

MAKE-UP AND HAIRDRESSING
Make-up Artist: Allen Weisinger
Assistant Make-up Artists: Peter Wrona Jr., Barbara Maggi
Hair Stylist: Joe Coscia
Assistant Hair Stylists: Stephen d'Amico, Romaine Green

EDITING AND DUBBING
Film Editor: John Bloom
Sound Editor: Jonathan Bates
Music Editor: Michael Tronick
Re-recording Mixers: Gerry Humphreys, Michael Minkler, Donald O. Mitchell, Kevin O'Donnell, Robin O'Donoghue
Assistant Film Editors: Jeremy Hume, Glenn Cunningham, Maryann Brandon, Kevin Lane, Ralph Sepulveda Jr.
Assistant Sound/Music Editors: Christopher Kennedy, Mick Monks, Emily Paine

MUSIC
Music: Marvin Hamlisch
Lyrics: Ed Kleban
Music arranged and conducted by: Ralph Burns
Dance music layouts: Joseph Joubert, Robert E. Wooten Jr.

PUBLICITY & CASTING
Director of Publicity: Diana (Carter) Hawkins
Casting by: Julie Hughes and Barry Moss, C.S.A
Additional Casting: Edward Blum
Unit Publicist: Vic Heutschy
Public Relations: Smith and Siegal
Publicity Assistant: Janet Weiss

PRODUCERS, WRITER, CHOREOGRAPHER & DIRECTOR
Executive Producer: Gordon Stulberg
Choreographer: Jeffrey Hornaday
Screenwriter: Arnold Schulman
Producers: Cy Feuer & Ernest H. Martin
Director: Richard Attenborough

Filmed in Panavision   Processed by Technicolor
Dolby Stereo
Filmed on location at the Mark Hellinger Theater, New York, NY and re-recorded at Twickenham Film Studios, England, and Goldwyn Sound Facility, Hollywood, Calif., USA.